PERFECT
PLATES

PERFECT

5

IN FIVE INGREDIENTS

PLATES

JOHN WHAITE

Photography by Helen Cathcart

Kyle Books

FOR WINNIE AND FDR

Acknowledgments

There are many people I would like to thank for help and advice over the years, but to ensure I don't heavily offend, I'm keeping this list of folk entirely relevant to this book. And I shan't gush, because I can't stand sickliness. So, in no particular order:

To: Kyle, Judith, Sophie, all at Kyle Books, Helen, Linda, River, Kinga, Nicole, Frances, Holly, Rosie, Jonny, Laura, and Paul.

"I can no other answer make but thanks, and thanks, and ever thanks."
William Shakespeare.

With love and gratitude.

Published in 2017 by Kyle Books
www.kylebooks.com

Distributed by National Book Network
4501 Forbes Blvd, Suite 200,
Lanham, MD 20706
Phone: (800) 462-6420
Fax: (800) 338-4550
customercare@nbnbooks.com

First published in Great Britain in 2016 by Kyle Books,
an imprint of Kyle Cathie Ltd

10 9 8 7 6 5 4 3 2 1

ISBN 978-1-909487-59-8

Designer: Paul Atkins
Photographer: Helen Cathcart
Food Stylist: Nicole Herft
Props Stylist: Linda Berlin
Project Editor: Sophie Allen
Editorial Assistant: Hannah Coughlin
Editorial Adaptation: Lee Faber
Production: Nic Jones, Gemma John, and Lisa Pinnell

Library of Congress Control Number: 2016956951

Color reproduction by ALTA, London
Printed and bound in China by 1010 International Printing Ltd.

The oven temperatures listed in this book are for standard ovens. If you have a fan-assisted or convection oven, simply decrease the temperature by about 35 degrees to achieve the same results.

CONTENTS

INTRODUCTION   06

MORNING PLATES   08

HEARTY PLATES   34

EVERYDAY PLATES   66

WORTH-THE-WAIT PLATES   94

POSH PLATES   114

MANY PLATES   146

SWEET PLATES   166

INDEX   206

INTRODUCTION

In all honesty, I was dreading writing this book. The premise of the title wasn't something I ever thought possible: that I could produce delicious meals with only a limited number of ingredients. In fact, the very thought filled me with horror; in my eyes, more is more, and I've never been one for frugality. You may wonder why I came up with the idea for this book. I too wondered that many a time over the course of the recipe testing, but as well as being a devout subscriber to immoderation, I am also a sucker for a challenge.

It transpired that my fears were entirely irrational: when I began to pare back recipes and use fewer ingredients, I was reminded of the uncomplicated flavors of my childhood. I remembered my Auntie Mary handing me a basket of cherry tomatoes. The smell of the tomatoes was so sweetly intense, that all they needed was a drizzle of peppery olive oil, and a few torn shreds of basil to complete them. It wasn't necessary to lob a load of other components thoughtlessly at the plate; it was unassumingly perfect in its simplicity.

That idea was something I wanted to return to, so the initial stage in writing this book was to define what perfection in food is. But to understand even that, I needed to ask myself: what is the ultimate aim of preparing food? Clearly, we've long since evolved from the primitive notion of "food as fuel." You only need to look to the abuse of food and vocabulary that is "molecular gastronomy" to know that today food is about entertainment. We throw dinner parties to entertain, as much as we do to catch up with friends, but let's face it, we all want to serve up an impressive spread, because we love a bit of glitzy one-upmanship on our peers.

Sometimes we cook for attention; chefs and cooks are often the most glory-hunting individuals on the planet. But surely you yourself can't deny that social praise for a toothsome batch of granola bars, brings an insatiable urge for more? My mother, in particular, is well versed in this little game. After a meal cooked by her, no matter how delicious it was, she would always apologise for "letting us down." She knows quite well how excellent her food is, but she loves us to make even more fuss over it. Poor Linda!

Really, I don't suppose the question of perfect food at home, on a day-to-day basis, is much considered in any depth. I think that's just because food is simply a part of who we are; it's a visceral appreciation. Food at home isn't perfect, and that is what is perfect about it. That's not to say that it is unconsidered, or taken for granted—though it can be—it's just that what we eat throughout our lives can, and does, depend heavily on what we are fed as children. We know what we enjoy, and that is something we can inherit. The food that we love stays with us as we grow up, without us really heralding or fussing over it all that much. I know that nothing I ever make for my partner will compare to his mother's corned beef hash—a fact that I have ambitiously, but futilely resisted for all too long.

For me, all of that highlights what perfect food is: simple ingredients that bring a reassuring familiarity, prepared with rustic sentiment. There's nothing elaborate needed; there's no urge to discover deeply complex flavors by way of lengthy processes, and specialist equipment—"imperfect plates," I guess, would have been a more suitable title for this book. There will always be the temptation to throw something else onto the plate, but you shouldn't be afraid to resist. Coco Chanel said that before you leave the house, you should remove one item of clothing. If anyone had ever tried to apply that concept to food, I'd have unfriended and blacklisted that person for life. But now, I completely get it: perfection is found in familiar simplicity.

The Premise and the Promise

This is a cookbook in which each recipe uses just five main ingredients. Your "free passes" are what I would call "the Essentials": oil, butter, salt, pepper, and water. They don't count in the five main ingredients, as I'd expect most people to already have them at home, in their cupboards and fridge.

Now, I'm sure we'd all love to spend our day trundling around an idyllic farmers' market, soaking up the sweet scent of vine tomatoes, and the boisterous pungency of towering stacks of artisan cheeses. I dream about testing ingredient after ingredient, revisiting each two or three times before deciding on my favorite, but that just isn't realistic; the scales of the work–life balance are most definitely dishonest. With that in mind, I've used ingredients here that are, for the most part, available in both supermarkets and specialist food markets. Both are fabulous, both are necessary, so the choice is entirely yours.

I'm stepping back from the currently complicated to let the ingredients do the talking; if we really needed all this elaborate molecular gastronomy, we'd have starved and shuffled off this mortal coil a long time ago.

With just five main ingredients, plates of food can be created. That is the premise. The promise is that the food will be perfect— not fancy, elaborate, or technical, just perfect.

MORNING PLATES

LAVISH WEEKEND BRUNCHES

Before you even begin to browse the recipes on the following pages, I feel the need to urge you to do so with the chapter's subtitle in mind: lavish weekend brunches. Many of the recipes here are decadent, but that's because they aren't intended to be something you'd eat every single morning. Well, you could, but who knows where that would get you? And besides, the origin of these indulgent recipes is rooted more in the social, joyous sort of breakfast rather than a lonesome, reluctant nibble on some stale cornflakes. You made it through the night—surely that's a reason to celebrate?

Joking aside, of course there are some more balanced recipes, too, and those are the ones that I make time and time again. It's just that I like to think weekend mornings are used properly. Throughout the week, most of us are frantic in our lives. We are slaves to the alarm clock, and the upward out-of-bed struggle is relentless. So when the weekend comes, I'd much rather have a lie-in, before I haul myself into the kitchen to calmly get on with some idle pottering.

What I'd truly like to do every weekend is spend an entire morning with friends or family, and food. I once went for brunch with a group of mates, and it lasted for five hours— admittedly, a bottomless supply of prosecco did fuel the fire, but that too can be arranged at home, can't it?

These recipes are the types of things you'd do as a breakfast buffet for your mates, as much as they are fitting treats for family brunches. However you view the recipes, and whatever occasion you cook them for, the real provenance of this entire chapter is found in that trite old cliché: breakfast is the most important meal of the day—because for me and mine, it truly is.

Banana and Blueberry Dutch Baby Pancake

SERVES
6 to 8

Bananas are a wonderfully sweet fruit, but when cooked, they become caramelized, and have a gentle toffee flavor. That said, this isn't a cloyingly sweet brunch dish; it's just about right, and the blueberries add a subtle sourness anyway. The batter is essentially a roasted pancake, so it couldn't be simpler.

---

3 large ripe bananas

---

6 tablespoons
self-rising flour

---

1 medium egg

⅔ cup whole milk

¾ cup blueberries

3½ tablespoons unsalted
butter

Preheat the oven to 425°F.

Slice the bananas lengthwise so you have 6 long halves. Place them into a medium-sized roasting dish (mine is 12 × 8 inches). Cube the butter, and scatter it over the bananas, cover them with foil, and then roast in the oven for 10 minutes.

Meanwhile, make the batter. Put the flour into a mixing bowl, and add the egg and 1½ tablespoons of the milk. Whisk to a thick, smooth paste, then slowly pour in the remaining milk, whisking constantly.

Once the bananas have had their 10 minutes, there will be a little moisture in the dish from the bananas; that's normal. Pour the batter over the bananas, then quickly scatter over the blueberries—I do this while the dish is still in the oven to ensure it stays hot, but don't risk burning yourself. Bake, uncovered, for 25 to 35 minutes, or until the batter has puffed up, and is a dark golden brown around the edges.

Variation
In place of the blueberries, raspberries work beautifully. And, rather than buy fresh, frozen berries work just as well, and there's no need to defrost them first.

Sausage, Kale, and Potato Casserole

When I asked around as to what brings people comfort, so many responded with "carbs and cheese." It's impossible to deny it: that combination has an instant warming and calming effect.

The added beauty of this is that you can prepare the entire thing a day in advance. Just assemble as detailed, then throw it into the fridge—get it out a good 30 minutes before you bake it, though.

With the sausages, I insist that you get the best quality you can, preferably those with a high mace or nutmeg content to bring an extra something to the dish.

SERVES
4 to 6

Preheat the oven to 400°F.

Into a mixing bowl, squeeze the meat out of the sausages, and discard the casing. Finely chop the kale—I also remove the thicker stalky bits—and add to the bowl. Heat 1 teaspoon olive oil in a skillet over medium–high heat, and add the meat and kale. Fry until the meat is cooked and slightly browned, then place into a clean mixing bowl.

Peel the potatoes, and coarsely grate them. Place the grated potato onto a clean, dry dishtowel or cheesecloth, and sprinkle 1 teaspoon salt all over them. Tightly squeeze the potatoes in the cloth to remove every last drop of moisture, then add to the pan, with another teaspoon of oil, and stir-fry until soft.

Add the cooked potatoes to the bowl with the kale and sausage meat. Grate the cheese, and add to the bowl. Season with 1 teaspoon black pepper and just a pinch more salt, then toss together until fairly evenly dispersed.

Beat the eggs in another bowl, then add to the potato mixture and stir together. Transfer to a pie dish or medium-sized enamel pan, and bake for 40 to 50 minutes, until golden brown and set. Remove from the oven, and allow to cool for 10 minutes before digging in.

1 pound fresh
link sausages

5½ ounces kale

1 pound russet or
Yukon gold potatoes

9 ounces extra sharp
Cheddar cheese
(or Emmental)

9 extra large eggs

olive oil, for frying
sea salt flakes
coarse black pepper

Cashew, Blackberry, and Maple Overnight Oats

This couldn't be simpler: just mix together the oats and milk in a bowl. Cover with plastic wrap, and refrigerate overnight.

In the morning, roughly chop the cashews, and halve the blackberries—though that could be done the night before, especially if you're one of those late risers who struggles to get ready and out of the door on time. Fold those into the oat mixture with the maple syrup and serve—you can add more milk, if it makes you happy.

Variation

You could swap the blackberries for any berry, and the cashews for any nut—this recipe is so versatile. And, of course, if you don't do dairy, almond or soymilk would work well.

scant 1½ cups rolled oats

2 cups milk, plus extra to serve (optional)

scant ½ cup cashews

1¼ cups blackberries

3 tablespoons maple syrup

Peanut Butter and Chocolate Chip Granola

MAKES 8 to10 PORTIONS

Preheat the oven to 300°F.

Place the oats in a large mixing bowl. In a saucepan, stir together the maple syrup and peanut butter over medium heat, until they mix together and become looser. Pour the maple syrup and peanut butter mixture over the oats, and stir until all of the oats are covered—the mixture will clump together into little nuggets, and that's exactly what you are looking for.

Scatter the mixture over a large baking sheet—you may need to do this on two baking sheets—and allow to dry out in the oven for 45 minutes, shaking the pans to mix everything up halfway through, so that the nuggets color evenly. Remove from the oven, and allow to cool and crisp on the baking sheets.

Chop the apricots into small chunks and toss them into the cooled granola with the chocolate chips, and stir through to distribute them evenly. Store in an airtight container or jar where it will last for a good 5 or 6 weeks.

4½ cups rolled oats

½ cup maple syrup

¾ cup crunchy peanut butter

1 cup dried apricots

⅔ cup dark chocolate chips

Nectarines with Thyme, Honey, and Strawberry Yogurt Cobbler

SERVES
2 to 4

Brunch doesn't have to be piles of pancakes and bacon (though that's never a negative thing), something a little lighter that sets you up for the day can be just as welcome. This—which is essentially a basic cobbler—is simple, yet satisfying at the breakfast table.

---

4 nectarines

---

5 teaspoons honey, plus a little extra to drizzle

---

3 sprigs of thyme (I use lemon or broad leaf)

¾ cup self-rising flour

---

scant ⅔ cup strawberry-flavored yogurt

---

sea salt flakes 1 tablespoon unsalted butter, at room temperature

---

Preheat the oven to 400°F.

Slice the nectarines in half, then carefully remove the pits—the best way is to very gently twist the two halves back and forth in opposite directions until loose enough that one half comes free from the pit. Remove the pit from the other half with a teaspoon, gently. Slice each half into four, and put into a roasting pan. Spoon over 2 teaspoons of the honey and toss together with the thyme.

For the topping, toss the flour in a mixing bowl with the smallest pinch of sea salt. Rub the butter into the flour until evenly dispersed and the flour resembles inelegant, yet fine bread crumbs. Pour the yogurt and remaining honey into the bowl and stir in—just until well amalgamated; you don't want to overmix this. The mixture should be very thick, but scoopable. Leave the dough to rest for 15 minutes, then spoon fairly even tablespoonfuls randomly over the nectarines.

Bake for 25 to 30 minutes, or until the nectarines are juicy and hot, and the topping has swollen and is a light golden-brown color. Serve warm.

Variation
Any soft, stone fruit would work well. Apricots would offer a little more sharpness, and so perhaps may need a bit more honey.

Crashed Breakfast Eggs

SERVES
2

I once ran away to Madrid where I fell in love, though really my love affair was with this dish. I ate it every day for brunch, and I make it so often now. The beauty of it is not only its simplicity, but also that it's a great recipe to experiment with—adding chorizo or pancetta in place of the sausage works particularly well. Traditionally, this is made with potatoes, but this version is a little lighter on the carbs.

3 best-quality fresh
link sausages

2 small bell peppers
(I use red and yellow)

4 scallions

4 extra large eggs

2 ounces Manchego
cheese

olive oil
sea salt flakes
coarse black pepper

Slice the sausages into ½-inch chunks. Seed and finely slice the peppers, chop the scallions into ½-inch pieces, and set aside until needed.

Heat 1 tablespoon olive oil in a skillet over high heat. Once the oil is hot, add the sausage chunks, turn the heat down to medium and fry for a good few minutes until cooked through, stirring them often. Add the peppers and scallions, and fry for a minute or so, just until softened.

Hold the eggs about 12 inches above the pan, and crack them open, allowing the insides to tumble and crash into the pan. Leave the eggs to fry for 2 minutes or so, until they are only just set. Grate the cheese and scatter it on top, then season to taste.

Maple-coated Bacon with Cinnamon Baked Apples

SERVES
4

Pork and apples: two ingredients that just go together without any question. This brunch version of the classic combination is slightly sweeter, and so more palatable when eaten first thing. The Granny Smiths are perfect here: not only are they sharp, and so suited to the candied bacon, but also they don't break down as much as other apple varieties when cooked. You're free to use whichever brand and style of bacon you prefer, but with the maple and cream cheese, I feel that American hickory smoked bacon is more fitting.

---

4 Granny Smith apples

½ teaspoon
ground cinnamon

---

8 slices hickory
smoked bacon

---

generous 2½
tablespoons
maple syrup

---

4 tablespoons
full-fat cream cheese

---

scant 3 tablespoons
unsalted butter, at room
temperature

Preheat the oven to 400°F.

Core the apples and slice them in half widthwise. Arrange them in a baking pan, and sprinkle with the cinnamon. Put a blob of butter onto each apple half.

Have a separate baking sheet ready for the bacon—though if you've got a wire rack that fits onto the baking sheet, use that, as it'll help to get the bacon crispy. Put the bacon into a mixing bowl, and rub the maple syrup into it as evenly as possible. Arrange the bacon, well spaced, on the baking sheet or rack, and pour over any remaining maple syrup.

Put everything into the oven and cook for 25 minutes. The apples should soften, but retain their shape, and the bacon should be crispy—if you like it really crispy, you may wish to leave it in the oven a little longer.

Serve the apples with a blob of cream cheese, and topped with the bacon—you can either chop it finely, or serve it as crispy slices.

Lady Grey Poached Prunes with Yogurt and Caramelized Oats

SERVES
4 to 6

Any fruit poached in syrup is bound to satisfy, but there's something particularly intriguing about the intense, almost molasses sweetness of prunes. The Lady Grey tea has a haunting bergamot-citrus flavor, which permeates into the syrup and prunes, and is so wonderful atop creamy, thick yogurt. Do go for the packages of dried prunes as opposed to the syrup-soaked variety; because the former are drier, they absorb much more of the poaching liquid.

6 Lady Grey (or Earl Grey) tea bags

¾ cup plus 3 tablespoons superfine sugar

2½ cups (1 pound) dried prunes

6½ tablespoons rolled oats

1¾ cups Greek yogurt

1¼ cups water

Put the water, tea bags and ¾ cup of the superfine sugar into a saucepan and bring to a boil. Reduce to a simmer and cook for 5 minutes, then add the prunes and return to a boil for just 1 minute. Remove from the heat, and allow to cool to room temperature. Once cooled, remove and discard the tea bags, then decant the prunes and syrup into a bowl, cover with plastic wrap, and leave overnight. If you prefer, you could decant them into a clean jar, and store them in the fridge for up to a month.

Heat a dry skillet over high heat. Once the pan is hot, add the oats, and toss them about in the pan for a minute or so to toast, then sprinkle in the remaining 3 tablespoons superfine sugar. Let the sugar caramelize and coat the oats, then tip out onto a plate, and allow to cool. If preparing in advance, store the oats in an airtight container with a slice of bread—the bread will hopefully soak up any humidity before the oats do.

To serve, simply pile the desired amount of prunes and their fruity tea syrup over a blob of yogurt, and top with the caramelized oats.

Rye Soda Bread with Egg Butter

MAKES
1 LOAF

Whenever I revel in the simplicity of making soda bread, I always feel as though I should crumble with guilt. For me, the idea of breadmaking conjures images of patience, but with soda bread, that waiting time is obliterated. This egg butter is to die for. It is common in eastern Finland, western Russia, and the bit in the middle: Karelia. And the saltier the butter, the better it is. The egg butter will keep in the fridge for up to a week.

scant 2½ cups
whole-wheat rye flour,
plus extra for dusting

2 teaspoons
baking powder

scant 1 cup buttermilk,
plus 2 tablespoons

5 extra large eggs

2 tablespoons dill

sea salt flakes
1½ sticks salted
butter, at room
temperature

For the bread, in a mixing bowl toss together the flour, baking powder, and 1 teaspoon sea salt. Rub 3 tablespoons of the butter into the flour until it comes together to form inelegant bread crumbs. Whisk together the scant 1 cup buttermilk and one of the eggs, then quickly but carefully mix this into the dry ingredients using a wooden spoon, to create a rough, scraggy mass. Once the mixture comes together, sprinkle a little flour onto the worktop, tip out the dough and work it—this isn't as vigorous as a kneading; it's more of a coaxing—until the dough comes together to form a ball. The dough will be fairly wet, so don't work it too much, just roll it into a ball.

Preheat the oven to 400°F.

Place the dough ball onto a baking sheet lined with parchment paper, pat it down lightly into a thick disc, and cut a deep cross into it—essentially, cut it into quarters barely attached at the bottom. Leave the loaf to rest at room temperature for just 20 minutes, then bake for 30 to 35 minutes, until crisp on the outside. This won't puff up anywhere near as much as an all-purpose flour soda bread, but that's absolutely fine—rye loaves are better that bit denser. Leave to cool on a wire rack.

For the egg butter, bring a medium saucepan of water to a boil. Add the remaining 4 eggs and boil for 8 minutes, then gently tip out the water and place them under cold running water. Once the eggs are cool enough to handle, peel them and chop them finely. Chop the dill finely, too, then mash together the eggs, remaining 1¼ sticks of butter, 2 tablespoons buttermilk, and the dill. To serve, slather the butter onto chunks of the bread.

Sweet Potato Hash with Egg, Pancetta, and Sage

We've all done it: had a little too much to drink the night before and woken up craving something savory, full of carbs and flavor. This really hits the spot. With a wedge of buttered bread, or toast on the side, it's worth the hangover. This doesn't need to be reserved solely for those mornings of regret though; it's a fairly balanced dish to kick-start any day.

about 2 medium
sweet potatoes
(10 ounces)

1 banana shallot

3 ounces pancetta or
smoked bacon cubes

2 sage leaves

1 extra large egg

sea salt flakes
heaping 1 tablespoon
unsalted butter
coarse black pepper

Bring a medium-sized saucepan of well-salted water to a boil. Meanwhile, peel the sweet potatos and chop into ½-inch cubes. Once the water is boiling, add the sweet potato chunks and bring back to a boil. Boil for 5 minutes, then drain.

Finely slice the shallot and set aside. Put the pancetta or bacon and butter into a skillet set over medium heat, and cook, stirring occasionally, for a good 5 minutes, until the pancetta fat renders down, then add the shallot, and allow that to soften.

Add the sweet potato cubes to the skillet and stir-fry for 1 to 2 minutes until heated through. Chop the sage finely, and stir through, then push the hash to the edge of the pan, and crack the egg into the center. Fry just until the white begins to set, then reduce the heat to low, and cover with a lid until the egg white is cooked, but the yolk is still runny. Remove from the heat, season, and savor.

Variation
If you're really hungover, try frying 4 ounces ground beef with the bacon and shallot for an extra hit of flavor. And, of course, you could use regular potatoes—go for russet.

Mushroom Stroganoff on Sourdough Toast

SERVES
1

When it comes to frying mushrooms, I'm an avid believer in Julia Child's method. She says not to overcrowd them in the pan, so that they fry rather than steam, so even with the small weight of mushrooms here, it's best to fry them in a few batches, so they don't go too soggy. The texture of these fried mushrooms is just right in this spicy, creamy sauce.

---

7 ounces mixed
mushrooms

---

1 teaspoon paprika

---

1 garlic clove

⅓ cup heavy cream

---

2 slices of
sourdough bread

---

scant 3 tablespoons
unsalted butter
sea salt flakes
coarse black pepper

If the mushrooms are a little grubby looking, give them a clean: use a clean, slightly damp cloth to wipe away any grit or dirt. Never wash mushrooms; their texture is like a sponge, and so will soak in any water and become waterlogged.

Melt the butter in a large skillet over medium-high heat. Slice the larger mushrooms finely, and add one-third of the mushrooms to the butter with a pinch of salt and pepper. Fry the mushrooms, stirring frequently, until they're colored—a good 5 minutes or more. Repeat with the remaining batches of mushrooms, then return all of the cooked mushrooms to the pan.

Add the paprika to the pan, stirring it through for just a minute. Mince the garlic, and add that along with the cream, and simmer for a few minutes until the mushrooms are coated in a paprika-flecked, thick sauce.

Toast the sourdough bread until crisp, then pile the mushroom stroganoff on top. Season to taste (I like a lot of pepper here) and serve.

Roasted Plum and
Goat Cheese Bruschetta

MAKES
2 PIECES

It's no secret that a tangy sweet something is the perfect accompaniment to a strong goat cheese. Add a crunchy wedge of sourdough to that combination, and well, that's pretty much success on a plate. It may seem a little odd to use plums, but actually, when they are roasted with the cinnamon and sugar, they turn into a sort of chunky chutney.

The night before, halve the plums and remove their pits, then slice each half in two—each plum should end up as four slices. Put the slices into a bowl, and toss with the sugar and cinnamon. Cover with plastic wrap, and set aside at room temperature.

The next morning, preheat the oven to 400°F. Space the plum pieces on a baking sheet, and roast for 20 minutes, or until cooked down and fairly limp.

Meanwhile, heat a grill pan over medium heat. Brush the slices of sourdough bread with a little olive oil. Fry the slices on both sides until delicately charred.

Spread the goat cheese over the charred sourdough, and top with a pile of the soft, sweet plums.

4 firm plums

2 tablespoons
superfine sugar

1 teaspoon
ground cinnamon

2 slices of
sourdough bread

4 ounces soft
goat cheese

Olive oil, for frying

Fried Lima Beans and Avocado

Having neglected to stock up on bacon and eggs before a night out with friends, the next morning we found ourselves ravenous and in need. All I had in were the ingredients for this dish—don't judge me, I'd only just moved in; my cupboards are ordinarily full to bursting.

This gives a somewhat healthier meaning to a "fried breakfast," but is still such a wholesome morning feast. The lima beans and avocado are both smooth and tender, but when you fry the beans this way, they become ever so slightly crispy on the outside. The trick to getting the most flavor is in slowly cooking the onions, so they caramelize and sweeten the dish.

SERVES
2

Peel and halve the onion, then slice it as finely as you can manage. In a skillet, heat half of the butter over low heat, and when the butter melts, add the sliced onion with a small pinch of salt and 1 teaspoon of the vinegar. Allow the onion to cook down very slowly, stirring occasionally, until mushy but not colored—about 20 minutes.

Once the onion is cooked, remove it from the pan and put it into a bowl. Drain the lima beans well. Peel and mince the garlic clove, and add it to the pan with the beans and remaining butter. Fry them over medium heat, tossing frequently, for 10 minutes, or until the beans are gently colored and tender.

Chop the avocado in half, remove the pit, and then scoop out the flesh and chop it roughly. Add it to the pan along with the onion. Fry for a couple of minutes more, then transfer to two plates. Sprinkle over a little more salt and pepper, if required, then drizzle over the remaining vinegar to taste.

1 medium red onion

about 4 teaspoons sherry vinegar

1 (15-ounce) can lima beans

1 garlic clove

1 ripe Hass avocado

3½ tablespoons unsalted butter
sea salt flakes
coarse black pepper

Affogato Monkey Bread

Monkey bread sounds fun, and it most certainly is. It's basically balls of pillowy white bread dough dipped into syrup and coated in sugar, then baked as a whole. Sort of like a very rough and ready share-and-tear loaf. My version—for an exceedingly indulgent brunch—is laced with coffee syrup, and served with ice cream, a combination inspired by the Italian classic, affogato.

scant 3 cups
bread flour

2½ teaspoons
(¼-ounce envelope)
active dry yeast
or instant yeast

scant 1 cup light
brown sugar

⅔ cup strong
black coffee

2 pints vanilla
ice cream

9 tablespoons (1⅛
sticks) unsalted butter,
plus extra for greasing
1⅛ cups water
sea salt flakes

Grease a 9-inch ring or savarin mold with butter.

I make the dough in my freestanding electric mixer fitted with a dough hook, but it can be made by hand. In a mixing bowl, toss together the flour with 1 teaspoon salt and the yeast. Add the water—room temperature is fine—along with 3½ tablespoons of the butter. Bring the ingredients together to a scraggy mass, then knead vigorously until elastic and smooth. This will take about 5 minutes on high speed in the mixer, or a good 10 minutes with full-throttle elbow grease by hand.

Bring the dough into a rough ball and place in the mixing bowl. Cover the bowl with plastic wrap, put in a warm place, and allow the dough to prove and rise until about doubled in size—up to an hour.

While the dough proves, make the syrup. Place the remaining 5½ tablespoons butter in a saucepan with 6½ tablespoons of the sugar and the black coffee. Stir everything together, then bring the contents of the pan to a boil. Boil for just a minute, stirring until well mixed. Remove from the heat and allow to cool a little. Put the remaining ½ cup sugar into a bowl.

When the dough has risen, gently slap it a couple of times to knock it back—a technical term for "deflate." Divide the dough into walnut-sized nuggets—about 30 to 35 in total. Roll each portion into a rough ball and dunk it into the coffee syrup, then into the sugar. Pile the dough balls into the prepared pan, and pour over 2 tablespoons of the syrup, reserving the rest for serving. Allow the dough to rise again, until it comes up to just under the rim of the pan, between 30 minutes and an hour.

Preheat the oven to 350°F.

Once the dough has risen, bake for 35 to 40 minutes until puffed up and golden brown. Invert the loaf immediately onto a wire rack, and allow to cool for about 15 minutes—you should serve this warm, but not so hot that the ice cream melts instantly. Boil the remaining syrup in a small saucepan until it's thick like honey.

Put the monkey bread onto a serving plate and pile the ice cream into the hole in the center. Drizzle over the syrup. Allow the eaters to tear off chunks of bread and scoop up loads of ice cream.

Variation

If you don't have a ring mold you could use a loaf pan instead, and serve slices of the bread topped with scoops of ice cream.

HEARTY PLATES

COMFORT FOODS

We all need comfort. It's part of the human condition to want to silence—or at least mute—the nagging of everyday life. Without wishing for this introduction to read like that of a DIY psychology manual, I feel, as we all do, that it's important to find a moment's peace in our hectic lives.

But comfort is unquestionably a personal thing. Even though we are gifted with empathy, it's impossible to measure those things that bring solace to one person against those of another. You may find a deep cosiness when wrapped in an oversized beach towel as the sun beams down on your toes. That's my idea of hell—sand in my sandwiches infuriates me. You might be most comforted when almost entirely submerged in a stiflingly hot bubble bath—with or without a rubber duck. Or you might just need a few quiet minutes to yourself, staring into blank space.

It's undeniable that for most people, certain foods will act as a consolatory cuddle; the phrase "comfort food" is internationally known for a reason. I like to think that there are times in every person's life when they need to put down the quinoa and indulge. Even some of the hardiest "eat-clean" folk I've come by (not that I strive to befriend such austere and ascetic souls) still search for something to enjoy on their "cheat day." Personally, I don't hold with that entire outlook, and I don't think anyone should categorize food as clean or unclean. Granted, some foods are richer in nutrients than others, but perhaps what those other foods lack in nutrient density, they make up for in reassuring comfort. That may seem like a superficial and convenient notion, but ask yourself this: can you deny that a pie of some form, with rich, flaky puff pastry, brings snuggly warmth? If you can deny that, fair enough, but I sincerely suggest you consciously uncouple yourself from this book and run it through your juicer. I should remind myself here that the pathway to comfort is a subjective one, of course.

It's important to achieve balance without the painstaking guilt that I see so many battle with. My mother says to me, "you can't have jam on your bread every day." Perhaps that's a little too frugal, but the metaphor works nonetheless: treats are spontaneous, and that's partly why we enjoy them so much.

The food in this chapter is wholesome, and not just because of the portion sizes, or the deeply satisfying ingredients, but because these dishes often play a part in the creation of warm memories, too. Whenever I reflect on a happy time, there's always been some hearty dish involved. Take my Haddock with Braised Chorizo and Leeks, for example: sheltering in my hotel from a bitterly cold winter in New York, I opted for something not too dissimilar. It worked. It brought me instant warmth. I find there are few minor troubles that a bowl of warming broth can't remedy.

Curried Romanesco and Tamarind Soup

SERVES
6 to 8

Romanesco, the spiky lime-green cousin of the standard cauliflower, is somewhat nuttier than the regular variety. It has such a great flavor, and as with any vegetable, once it is roasted, that flavor amplifies. Roasted cauliflower on its own or as a side dish is delicious (see my Spiced Wine Brisket with Roasted Cauliflower on page 111), but when you take that intensified taste and add it to a few other ingredients, you get something so complex and wonderful.

Tamarind is the very tangy fruit from the tamarind tree, which can be processed into either dense blocks or paste. Both are readily available in larger supermarkets (usually on the world or foreign food aisles) and, of course, online.

Preheat the oven to 425°F.

**1¼ pounds
Romanesco cauliflower**

1 large red onion

**2 tablespoons
curry powder**

**4½ cups good-
quality chicken or
vegetable stock**

**2 tablespoons
tamarind paste**

olive oil, for roasting
sea salt flakes
coarse black pepper

Chop the cauliflower into large florets—and don't neglect the stalk, which has so much flavor. Peel the onion, and cut it into quarters, leaving the root end intact so the individual layers don't flake apart and burn, though do shave off the thread-like roots with a sharp knife. Place the cauliflower pieces and onion in a roasting pan and add 3 tablespoons of olive oil, the curry powder and 1 teaspoon each of salt and pepper. Toss together so that everything is well coated, then roast for 20 to 25 minutes, or until the cauliflower just starts to char, and the onion is fairly soft.

While the vegetables roast, bring the stock to a boil in a large saucepan, but don't leave it boiling; just get it hot, then remove from the heat. Once the vegetables have cooked, add them to the stock, cover with a lid, and simmer for 10 minutes. After this time, remove a ladleful of the cauliflower florets, for decoration, then blitz the rest until smooth—either in batches in a food processor, or with a handheld stick blender.

Return the soup to the saucepan, and stir in the tamarind paste. Check the seasoning, adding more salt and pepper if necessary, then serve with the reserved florets of cauliflower on top.

As with most soups, this freezes just fine and will keep for a good six months in an airtight container, or portioned in ziplock bags. Defrost and reheat thoroughly before serving.

Sweet Potato and Lentil Red Curry Soup

It's as though sweet potatoes and lentils were divinely created especially for soups and curries. They swell, and so bulk the dish, but they also absorb flavors: each sip of this soup is spiked with the spiciness from the paste, balanced with the sweetness of the potato. The sharp tang from the lime brings out every element of flavor.

SERVES
6 to 8

Peel the sweet potatoes and chop them into ½-inch cubes. Rinse the lentils in a strainer under cold running water until the water runs clear.

Heat a large saucepan or Dutch oven—one you have a lid for— over high heat. Add the red curry paste, and stir-fry for just 1 minute, until it becomes strongly aromatic. Quickly add the potato and lentils, and stir to coat in the paste, then pour in the stock. Bring the contents of the pan to a boil, then reduce to a very gentle simmer, and cook with the lid on for 35 to 40 minutes, just until the lentils and sweet potato are soft.

Ladle the soup into a food processor, and blitz until smooth and thick. Return to the pan, and add a generous pinch of pepper and a pinch of salt, if required. Add the lime juice, and stir in before serving.

As with most soups, this freezes just fine and will keep for a good six months in an airtight container, or portioned in ziplock bags. Defrost and reheat thoroughly before serving.

Leftover ingredient
Use leftover red curry paste for the Red Curry Sea Bass with Potato Rosti on page 131.

about 3 medium sweet potatoes (generous pound)

2 cups split red lentils

3 heaping tablespoons red curry paste

6¼ cups good-quality stock (I use beef, but it's your choice)

juice of 2 limes

coarse black pepper
sea salt flakes

Garlic, Anchovy, and Olive Flatbreads

MAKES
4

During a walk with my dad one spring, we came across a forest floor of wild garlic (ramps). The little white flowers floating above a thick sea of green leaves had an aroma that was so intense—somewhere between garlic and chive. With the find, we made these flatbreads.

Because wild garlic is seasonal, and seemingly never sold in supermarkets, this recipe uses normal garlic. It's actually an improvement on the original: it's strong enough to retain its own flavor alongside the boisterous hit from the anchovies, which slightly overwhelmed the wild garlic. The beer is used to make the dough itself mainly for flavor. It brings a gentle, fermented depth to the flatbreads, making them even more savory and satisfying.

1½ cups self-rising flour, plus extra for dusting

4⅓ cups beer

---

4 anchovies from a jar

---

8 pitted green olives

---

4 large garlic cloves

sea salt flakes
6 tablespoons olive or canola oil

To make the bread, simply mix the flour with 1 teaspoon salt and the beer. Bring together into a rough dough, then knead on the worktop for a few minutes, or until smooth. Leave the dough in the bowl, and cover with plastic wrap to rest for 15 minutes.

For the topping, roughly chop the anchovies and olives, and mince the garlic. Add to a saucepan with the oil, and sauté over low heat for 1 minute. Remove from the heat, and leave the flavors to infuse into the oil.

Divide the dough equally into four. On a lightly floured worktop, roll out each portion of dough to a circle about 8 inches in diameter. Heat a dry skillet over high heat, and once it is hot, add the flatbreads, one at a time, and fry for a minute, or until the topside becomes slightly bumpy. Flip the flatbread over, and fry the other side for a minute or so more. You don't want the flatbreads to be burnt, but there's nothing wrong with a few bits of char. If you're cooking on gas, remove the flatbread from the pan—with kitchen tongs—and place it directly onto the flame for 10 seconds. It should swell up slightly. Remove from the heat, and stack the flatbreads onto a plate.

Top each flatbread with the infused oil and serve.

Hummus, Pepper, and Gorgonzola Flatbread Pizza

MAKES
1 LARGE
PIZZA

This may at first seem a bizarre combination of ingredients, and I suppose it is, but it just works. It's based on the pizzas I used to enjoy at the Grinch wine bar in Manchester. Sadly, it's no longer there, but this pizza perpetuates its memory.

Although the pizza base isn't an authentic one (there's no yeast used), it works very well, but only if the oven is hot enough; the key to any pizza is to ensure the oven is at a ferocious heat. That, and so you have a hot base to slide the raw pizza onto—a pizza stone, or a strong baking sheet heated in the oven works perfectly.

1⅓ cups self-rising flour, plus extra for dusting

---

2 tablespoons hummus

---

4 roasted peppers from a jar

3½ ounces Gorgonzola dolce cheese

---

2 teaspoons sweet chili dipping sauce

---

sea salt flakes
⅔ cup water
olive oil

Preheat the oven to 500°F, and place a pizza stone, or a strong, large baking sheet in the oven to get hot.

Toss together the flour with ½ teaspoon salt, then add the water and a glug (about 1 tablespoon) of olive oil. Bring together into a dough, and knead for a couple of minutes until smooth. Ball up the dough and leave it in the mixing bowl to soften for 20 minutes, at room temperature.

Once the dough has rested, lightly flour the worktop and roll the dough out into a large, thin circle—if the base is left too thick, it won't crisp up, and will stay doughy and soggy. Slide the pizza base onto a well-floured baking sheet. Spread the hummus over the pizza base, then tear the peppers into long strands and scatter them over the top. Crumble on the Gorgonzola, then slide the pizza onto the hot pizza stone or baking sheet, and cook for 7 to 10 minutes, until slightly colored, and very crispy around the edges.

Drizzle the baked pizza with the chili sauce and serve. You can slice this into neat portions with a pizza wheel, but I like to embrace its flatbread origins, and just tear off pieces.

Note

The hummus works so well because it is thick and doesn't make the base soggy. I wouldn't recommend using a tomato sauce for the base, unless the sauce is extremely thick.

Garlicky, Cheesy, Giant Hasselback Potatoes

There is hardly anything cosier than a baked potato. It's all in the simple perfection of it: crispy, golden skin, encasing a fluffy, buttery interior. Whether served with baked beans, cheese, or whatever else you prefer, it is a staple—something we may take for granted until the moment we dig in again, when the troubles of the outside world are silenced, even if only for a moment.

This version marries my favorite spud preparation— hasselback potatoes from Sweden—with those buttery beauties that I've relied on for decades.

MAKES
2

Preheat the oven to 375°F.

Clean the potato skins, if necessary, then cut deep slashes into them, but don't cut all the way through. The best way to ensure you don't mess it up, is to pop the potato between two wooden spoon handles, and with a sharp knife slice down until the handles prevent you from cutting any deeper.

Finely chop or mince the garlic, and add it to a saucepan with the butter and Worcestershire sauce. Heat over high heat, stirring, just until the butter melts completely. Pour the melted butter over the potatoes, spreading the slices open as you pour. Bake, uncovered, for 1½ to 2 hours, until golden brown and crispy.

Remove the potatoes from the oven and tear the Camembert into small chunks, slotting them in the crevices in the potatoes along with the rosemary. Return the spuds to the oven for just 5 minutes, or until the cheese has melted.

---

2 large baking potatoes

---

4 garlic cloves

---

2 teaspoons Worcestershire sauce

3½ ounces Camembert cheese

---

2 sprigs of rosemary

½ stick unsalted butter
sea salt flakes
coarse black pepper

Sweet Potato, Gruyère, and Pecan Gratin

SERVES
4 to 6

This is a dish that proves you don't always need meat to make a meal. I'm a devout carnivore myself, so you can rest assured that I'm not trying to indoctrinate you with veg-only ways. The nuttiness from the Gruyère and the pecans goes brilliantly with the sweet and earthy potato.

2¾ lb sweet potatoes

1¾ cups heavy cream

sprig of rosemary

3½ ounces
Gruyère cheese

½ cup pecans

butter, for greasing
sea salt flakes
coarse black pepper

Preheat the oven to 400°F. Grease a 9-inch (approx.) pie dish (ceramic is best) with butter. Whatever you do, don't use a dish with a loose bottom, or you'll be scrubbing your oven floor for weeks.

Peel the sweet potatoes and slice each very thinly—I use a mandoline or a food processor, but it can be done using a knife, with a straight eye, and steady hand. After you've sliced each potato, rearrange the slices as though you were trying to stick them back together to reform the whole potato. Wedge these bundles into the greased dish randomly and at different angles—treat them as though the potatoes were whole, just packing them tightly into the dish.

Heat the cream in a medium saucepan over low heat. Add the rosemary with a pinch of salt and pepper. Once the cream comes to a simmer, remove from the heat, and leave to infuse for 5 minutes.

Pour the infused cream over the waiting sweet potato. Cover the dish with foil, and bake for 45 minutes, then remove from the oven and take off the foil.

Coarsely grate the cheese, and roughly chop the pecans, then scatter both cheese and nuts over the baked gratin. Return to the oven for an additional 15 to 20 minutes, until the cheese top is bronzed, and the sauce is bubbling. Allow to cool and set for 15 minutes before diving in.

Variations
You could try using regular potato with Stilton or Cheddar. If you're not keen on rosemary, exchange it for thyme.

Haddock with Braised Chorizo and Leeks

I adore the somewhat contradictory delicate boldness of smoked fish. A newcomer might suspect that the delicate flesh wouldn't take the flavor, but we all know that it just works. That gentle smokiness pairs so well with the paprika-spiked chorizo. The tender leeks and slightly startling bite from the capers elevate the flavor of this dish—which is essentially a broth—even further.

SERVES
2 to 4

Preheat the oven to 400°F.

Cut the chorizo into ¼-inch slices. Slice the leeks into ½-inch discs, and set aside until needed.

Heat a heavy, shallow Dutch oven—one you have a lid for—over high heat, and add the chorizo. Fry the pieces, stirring every few seconds, until the chorizo starts to leak out its orange, spicy oil. Once it does, add the leeks to the pan and fry for 1 minute. Add the stock with a pinch of salt and pepper, bring to a boil, then cover with the lid, and cook for 40 minutes in the oven—if you don't have a lid, a piece of foil tightly wrapped around the rim of the pan should be ok.

After 40 minutes, uncover the pan and lay the haddock fillets on top. Return the pan to the oven and cook for an additional 10 to 12 minutes, until the haddock is cooked through. Flake the haddock into the broth beneath, scatter over the capers, check the seasoning—though I find this to be balanced enough—and, finally, serve.

10½ ounces raw chorizo sausage

2 large leeks

2¼ cups good-quality chicken stock

2 large smoked haddock fillets (I prefer undyed)

2 tablespoons non-pareil capers

sea salt flakes
coarse black pepper

Chorizo and Chickpeas Braised in Cider

**SERVES
2**

Chubby chickpeas are marvelous. They are surprisingly meaty, and have such a smooth, buttery inside. For that reason I'd always opt for the slightly more pricey jarred varieties, as those in cans can sometimes be very tough.

This flavor combination is not new—I had chorizo cooked in cider quite a few times when I spent a summer in Madrid—but it's here to stay. An interesting alternative to cider would be sherry. I've tried it both ways, and loved them both, but I'm a sucker for that sweet sharpness that cider brings.

9 ounces raw
chorizo sausage

3 cups drained
chickpeas from a jar

⅓ cup good-quality
beef stock

scant 1 cup dry
hard cider

Small handful of
flat-leaf parsley

olive or canola oil
sea salt flakes
coarse black pepper

In a large sauté pan, heat a good glug of oil over medium heat. Chop the chorizo sausages into ¼-inch thick discs, and add them to the pan. Fry the chorizo, stirring occasionally, for about 5 minutes, or until cooked through and just starting to brown.

Add the chickpeas to the pan, and stir to coat, then add the stock and hard cider. Bring to a boil, then reduce the temperature to a gentle simmer, and cook slowly to reduce, until the liquid in the pan is sparse and thick. Remove from the heat, and season to taste.

Roughly chop the parsley and scatter over the top to serve.

Variations
While chickpeas are best for this dish, you could use those gorgeous, plump lima beans from a jar instead.

Taleggio and Sausage Mac 'n' Cheese

SERVES
4 to 6

One of the world's ultimate comfort foods, Mac 'n' Cheese is gooey, rich, and fulfilling. Here I've used an Italianate pairing: the fennel-flecked salsiccia sausages, which are so bold in flavor, and the creamy, yet tangy Taleggio cheese. The real trickery in this dish, though, is that the traditional béchamel sauce is substituted with evaporated milk, making cozy indulgence an even quicker feat.

6 Italian fennel sausages

12 ounces small pasta (I use fusilli bucati/rotini)

1¾ cups canned evaporated milk

14 ounces Taleggio cheese

4½ ounces mozzarella cheese

sea salt flakes
coarse black pepper

Preheat the oven to 425°F.

Place the sausages into a medium-sized roasting dish (use the one you plan to cook the finished dish in, so that it keeps the flavors). Once the oven is hot, cook the sausages for 25 to 30 minutes, until gently colored and cooked through. Remove from the roasting dish and allow to cool—but leave all of those meaty juices in the dish.

Meanwhile, bring a saucepan of water to a boil, and add a few generous pinches of salt. Add the pasta, and boil for 9 minutes. Drain, leaving the pasta in the strainer or colander until required.

Reduce the oven temperature to 400°F. Once the sausages are cool enough to handle, slice them into fairly thick chunks.

Using the same pan, bring the evaporated milk to a simmer, and add the Taleggio in chunks. Stir the sauce until the cheese melts, and everything is smooth. Stir in 1 teaspoon black pepper and a pinch of salt to taste, then add the pasta and sliced sausages, stirring well to coat everything.

Pour the mac 'n' cheese into the roasting dish. Tear over the mozzarella, and bake for 35 to 40 minutes, until the sauce is bubbling, and the mozzarella is molten and burnished.

Variations
If you can't get hold of the Italian sausage, go for a good-quality sausage that contains fennel (fresh or seeds). If you can't find Taleggio, use a strong Brie or Camembert instead.

Rice Krispie-coated Chicken Tenders with Stilton Sriracha Sauce

The idea of coating chicken in breakfast cereal may seem fairly childish, but actually the results are so pleasing. And besides, cornflakes are used a lot for coating chicken, so I refuse to be embarrassed by this recipe. With the pungent and piquant dip, this is such a comforting treat.

SERVES
4

In a mixing bowl, combine the chicken tenders with ½ cup of the buttermilk so that each piece is very well coated. Cover with plastic wrap, and refrigerate for one hour—or leave it overnight if you can, as the chicken will then be incredibly tender.

Add a generous pinch of salt and pepper to the chicken bowl, mixing well, then dredge each piece of chicken through the Rice Krispies until very well coated.

Pour ½-inch (depth) of oil into a deep-sided skillet or sauté pan, and heat over medium–high heat. Once the oil is hot, add the chicken tenders, and fry for a few minutes on each side, until golden brown and cooked through. If they darken a little too quickly, your oil is too hot. Place the cooked pieces onto a plate lined with a couple of layers of kitchen towels to drain off the excess grease.

For the sauce, put the remaining buttermilk into a food processor with the Stilton and Sriracha, and blitz to a smooth dip.

Allow the chicken tenders to cool just until you can manage to gobble them up without burning your mouth, then serve with the sauce for dipping into.

1¼ pounds boneless, skinless chicken breast tenderloins (or just cut 1¼ pounds boneless, skinless chicken breasts into smaller chunks)

1¼ cups buttermilk

6 cups Rice Krispies cereal

8 ounces blue Stilton cheese, at room temperature

½ cup Sriracha chili sauce

sea salt flakes
coarse black pepper
oil, for frying

Alternative cooking option
For a slightly lighter version, try roasting the coated chicken tenders at 400°F for 25 minutes; though they'll not be as dark or as crispy.

Sticky Black
Sesame Chicken

SERVES
4

Let's face it, a big bowl of white rice and sticky sweet chicken can never see us wrong. This dish is certainly comforting, but it is so in an intriguing way. The honey brings the sticky sweetness and the dark soy sauce isn't salty like the lighter version—instead it is caramelized and full-bodied. I prefer black sesame seeds here for the dark color, but you could use whichever you prefer.

3½ tablespoons dark
soy sauce, plus extra
to serve (optional)

5⅔ tablespoons
black sesame
seeds, plus extra to
serve (optional)

scant ½ cup
clear honey

8 skinless, boneless
chicken thigh fillets

10½ ounces
basmati rice

sea salt flakes
olive oil

Preheat the oven to 400°F.

Place the soy sauce, sesame seeds, and honey into a small saucepan, and bring to a boil. Boil for a few minutes until well mixed, then add a pinch of salt and stir through.

Place the chicken thighs into a roasting dish, and pour over the sauce. Coat the chicken pieces well, then roast for 30 minutes, uncovered.

While the chicken roasts, cook the rice. Rinse the rice well in a strainer under cold running water until the water runs clear. Tip the rice into a saucepan, and cover with water—you need it to be a good ¾ inch above the surface of the rice. Add a pinch of salt and 1 tablespoon oil, then bring the pan to a boil. Once it is boiling, reduce the heat to low, cover the pan with a lid, and gently cook the rice for 10 minutes. Remove from the heat—don't even think about taking the lid off— and leave to rest for a good 10 minutes more.

Leave the chicken in the roasting dish, and pour the sauce into another saucepan. Bring the sauce to a boil, and reduce it until it's a little thicker and stickier. Pour it back over the thighs, then serve the sticky chicken over the rice, and do feel free to add extra soy sauce and sesame seeds.

Cozy Roasted Chicken and Green Lentils

SERVES
4

A roast chicken, done properly, is the epitome of comfort food for me. There's nothing I love more than the smell of a bird roasting: a mouthwatering premonition of the bronzed beauty itself, which later comes steaming from the oven.

To capitalize on the chicken's juices, I set the lentils beneath the bird, so that every last drop of fat falls down and bastes them, making a flavorsome broth. That's why a roasting dish with one of those elevated racks is necessary here. If you were to just drop the chicken on top of the lentils, the underside of the bird would remain pale, and I want every last inch to be golden.

2 leeks

2 celery stalks

scant 1¼ cups
dried green lentils

1 roasting chicken
(approx. 3¾ pounds)

1 head of garlic

3¾ cups boiling water
⅓ cup unsalted butter
sea salt flakes
coarse black pepper

Preheat the oven to 500°F.

Finely slice the leeks and celery and place in a roasting pan—one you have a rack for—with the lentils. Toss everything together, and add a pinch of salt and pepper. Add 3 cups of the boiling water.

Untruss the chicken and discard the giblets—or freeze them, as I do, ready for a rainy day of stock-making. Soften the butter so that it is malleable, but not melted. Repeatedly pinch the skin of the chicken breast to loosen it, then at the neck end, carefully work your hand between the skin and the breast meat. Once you have loosened the skin, take half of the softened butter, and slide it in between the meat and skin on each breast. Spread the remaining butter over the skin of the entire chicken, and season with a pinch of salt and pepper. Place the chicken onto the rack, so that it is elevated above the lentils. Halve the garlic and stuff it into the chicken cavity.

Put the pan into the oven, and immediately reduce the temperature to 400°F. Roast for 30 minutes, then add the remaining water to the lentils—if you can do this without taking the pan out of the oven, do so. Roast for 1 hour longer, or until the chicken is golden brown and cooked through—when you slice into the crease at the top of the leg, the juices should run clear; if they don't, roast for a little longer. The lentils will be a little dry-looking on top, but when you stir them, they'll be deliciously tender.

Serve platefuls of the lentils topped with thick slices of the chicken, or you could plonk the whole pan on the table and dig in—though do get in there before anyone else can; it's every man for himself when a roast is involved.

Chicken, Leek and Cider Mug Pot Pies

SERVES
4 to 6
(depending on
the mug size)

As I write this introduction, I can't help but giggle at my mom's comments about this recipe. When I handed a pie to her on a blustery autumn day, she dug in, and without so much as a thank you, said in her Northern accent, "Oh love, there's a lot of leek in here." But that's the point: lots of leeks, because I love them—especially when they are sweetly caramelized, and mixed with dry hard cider.

---

18 ounces boneless, skinless chicken thighs

---

14 ounces leeks (about 4)

1¾ cups dry hard cider

---

scant ½ cup full-fat crème fraîche

---

12 ounces packaged ready-rolled puff pastry sheets

---

olive oil, for frying
sea salt flakes
coarse black pepper
3½ tablespoons unsalted butter

Chop the chicken into ¾-inch nuggets. Wash and trim the leeks (if not already prepared), and slice into thin discs.

Heat a fairly large saucepan over high heat, and add a glug of oil. Once the oil is hot, add the chicken pieces with a pinch of salt and pepper, and fry until all sides are more or less seared. Remove from the pan, and put into a bowl, setting aside until needed.

Put the leeks into the same pan with the butter, and another pinch of salt and pepper, and reduce the heat to low. Allow the leeks to caramelize very slowly, stirring occasionally— this will take a good 20 minutes or so. Once the leeks have cooked down, return the chicken to the pan, and pour over the cider. Increase the heat to bring the contents of the pan to a boil, then reduce to a simmer, and cook, uncovered, for 45 minutes—you want the cider to evaporate just a little. Remove the pan from the heat, and allow to cool.

Preheat the oven to 400°F.

Once the filling has cooled, add the crème fraîche and more salt and pepper to taste, and stir until well mixed. Divide the mixture between 4 to 6 ovenproof mugs or ramekins.

For the pastry top, unroll the pastry and cut out discs that are just a little bigger than the mugs, and place them over the filling, tucking the excess pastry around the edge of the mug. Bake the pies for 30 to 35 minutes, until the pastry is golden brown and puffed.

Variation
Rather than making six small pies, you could put the filling mixture into an enamel pie dish, and bake it as one large pie.

Eastern Spiced Meatballs with Fiery Tomato Soupy Sauce

Some like it hot—and I most certainly do. That's something you'll praise or curse me for when you're tucking into this. Obviously, you can reduce the four chiles to just one if you like something milder, but I love how fiery it all is. The addition of butter in the sauce does help to temper the heat somewhat, but the main goal with that is to make it into a velvety, voluptuous sauce—almost like the canned cream of tomato soup I enjoyed as a child.

The meatballs are roasted rather than fried. Not only does that make the whole thing easier, but it also ensures the meatballs roast rapidly and so stay succulent.

SERVES
2

Preheat the oven to 425°F.

Quarter the tomatoes, and put them, along with the chiles, onto a baking sheet—make sure they aren't huddled together, otherwise the excess liquid won't evaporate. Sprinkle with a pinch of salt, and leave to macerate at room temperature.

For the meatballs, put the ground beef into a mixing bowl and add the spices with ½ teaspoon salt, 1 teaspoon pepper, and 3 tablespoons olive oil. Mix everything together until it's paste-like—I use my hands—then divide into 16 portions, rolling each into a compacted ball. Put the meatballs onto another baking sheet or roasting pan.

Put the sheet of tomatoes and chiles into the oven, and roast for 15 minutes, then add the meatballs to the oven, and roast everything for an additional 10 to 12 minutes. As soon as the meatballs are cooked through, transfer them to a plate, and cover with foil. If the tomatoes don't look slightly charred and limp, leave them in the oven until they do.

For the sauce, remove and discard the stalks from the roasted chiles, and put the chiles, along with the tomatoes, into a small food processor (I use my NutriBullet), along with the juices from the meatball pan and the butter. Blitz to a smooth sauce, then serve in bowls, with the meatballs studded on top, and dusted with a light sprinkling of allspice and cinnamon.

1½ pounds vine tomatoes

---

4 fat red chiles

1½ pounds ground beef (at least 15% fat)

---

1 heaping teaspoon ground allspice, plus extra for sprinkling

---

½ teaspoon ground cinnamon, plus extra for sprinkling

---

sea salt flakes
coarse black pepper
olive oil
2 tablespoons unsalted butter

Cheeseburger Quesadillas

SERVES
4

I was, at first, slightly embarrassed by this recipe; it just seemed a little too gratuitous to be included in a cookbook. But after eating my way through an entire batch of these (seriously!) I decided I couldn't leave it out. Especially not from the comfort food chapter: these are too gooey, too toothsome, and they are most certainly too comforting, to be kept as a dirty little secret. And even better, these are doubly indulgent: not only are they stuffed with fried beef and cheese, but the oil from the beef is also used to paint the tortilla before it goes onto the grill pan.

26 ounces ground
beef (at least 15% fat)

4 spicy dill pickles
from a jar

4 white corn tortillas

14 ounces sharp
Cheddar cheese

4 tablespoons
yellow mustard, plus
extra for dunking

olive oil
sea salt flakes
coarse black pepper

Heat 2 tablespoons oil in a large skillet over high heat, and once it is hot, add the ground beef with a generous pinch of salt and plenty of pepper. Stir-fry the beef for a minute or two, until colored and cooked through. Remove from the heat, and put the meat into a bowl—though leave all of the meaty juices in the pan, as these will come in handy.

Heat a dry grill pan over medium-low heat. Take a tortilla and place a quarter of the beef over half of the tortilla. Slice a quarter of the pickle, and scatter over the beef, then coarsely grate the cheese and scatter over a quarter of it. Spread 1 tablespoon mustard over the exposed half of tortilla, then fold the tortilla in half, encasing the filling.

Using a pastry brush or your fingertips, paint the uppermost side of the tortilla with the juices from the pan, then flip it into the griddle pan and paint the other side with more juices. Hold the quesadilla down with a spatula for a minute or so until crispy on one side, and marked by the pan, then flip it over and cook for an additional minute or two—you want the cheese to be absolutely molten, and the tortilla to be crispy.

Repeat with the remaining ingredients.

EVERYDAY PLATES

SIMPLE DISHES

Now, what I'm about to tell you might come as a shock, but here goes: you don't need to iron your clothes; your body will iron them for you. It saddens, no, infuriates me, to hear tales of skipping any sort of homemade dinner in favor of a gas-station sandwich just because there's ironing to be done. And don't get me started on those supermarket-foraged frozen dinners; though, admittedly, there must be a certain stress-relieving quality in the repeated stabbing of a plastic seal. But that is all they're good for, and I'm not falling foul to food snobbery—I just have to draw the line somewhere.

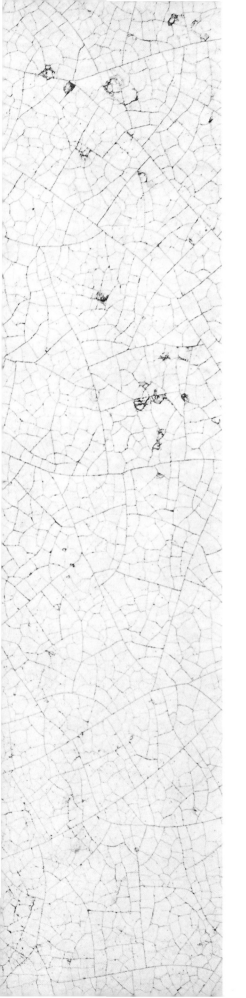

For me, there's no place I'd rather be than in my kitchen, stirring delicious concoctions in pots and pans; though I appreciate that I am lucky enough to do that for a living, so my entire day is spent propping up the stove. That doesn't mean I don't have a stressful job, though, because, believe me, I do, but my oven is my office. And nor do I have the responsibility of child rearing, or having to face a treacherous commute day-in, day-out. I am aware there is life beyond the stove—though I'm not quite ready to accept that yet—so these recipes will slot snugly into a busy lifestyle.

The point I'm trying to make is this: the recipes in this chapter are quick or simple to prepare, and that doesn't mean there will be a sacrifice of flavor or quality. In fact, these dishes didn't originate with time-saving in mind. Some of them aren't so much fast-cooked recipes as fuss-free. The primary objective here is that these meals are delicious and fresh, but they just happen to be easy or quick to prepare, too. Serendipity, you may call it.

My initial worry when naming this chapter was that the everyday emphasis might conjure up images of the trite, regimented meals done time and time again. Don't get me wrong, I love a chili con carne on a Wednesday as much as the next person, but I want to offer something different, something exciting. The meals in this chapter use the regular, everyday staple ingredients (salmon fillets and sausages, etc.), but they're reinvigorated with more rousing, impactful flavors. And don't worry, because these extra, more interesting ingredients are just as readily available.

Roasted Zucchini and Tomatoes with Mozzarella and Basil

SERVES
4

A great benefit to zucchini is how juicy they are. When you roast them, that juice partly evaporates, so that not only does the flavor intensify, but it thickens somewhat, too. This makes for an almost self-dressing salad, even more so when paired with the tangy, sweet tomatoes. Plum tomatoes, generally, have thicker flesh and less juice, so are perfect here.

---

14 ounces baby zucchini

---

8 ounces baby plum tomatoes

---

1 small red onion

---

9 ounces good-quality mozzarella cheese

---

12 large basil leaves

---

olive oil
sea salt flakes
coarse black pepper

Preheat the oven to 425°F.

Halve the zucchini lengthwise, and put them into a roasting pan along with the tomatoes. Add 2 tablespoons olive oil and a pinch of salt and pepper. Peel the onion, and cut it into thin wedges, adding those to the pan—the easiest way is to keep the root intact, so the layers of each wedge don't fall apart. Toss everything together, and roast for 25 to 30 minutes, until the tomatoes are slightly shriveled, and the zucchini are soft. Allow to cool completely in the pan, then transfer to a serving bowl.

Once the veg has cooled, tear the mozzarella into small nuggets and throw into the veg. Roll up the basil leaves in between your palms, clap your hands together to bruise the basil and release the flavor, then tear it into the salad. Toss everything together, add a little more oil and salt if you feel it necessary, and serve.

Variation
If baby zucchini aren't in season, just use the same weight of regular zucchini and chop them into large chunks—perhaps in half lengthwise, and then each half into three or four sizeable pieces.

Make in Advance
Because this is served at room temperature, it could be made up to 3 days in advance and kept in the fridge. Though in that case I wouldn't add the basil, extra oil, and salt until an hour before serving.

Rustic Mediterranean Tomato Tart

SERVES
8

The vibrant color of mixed heirloom tomatoes is awesome; there is a whole palette to choose from. I particularly love the green tigers, with their verdant skin and dark green stripes and those tiny little yellow ones with a zingy, sharp flavor.

This tart is gorgeous served slightly warm, but I prefer it once it has cooled completely. The flavors just seem to have found one another by the time it has come to room temperature.

12 ounces packaged
ready-rolled puff
pastry sheets

3½ ounces soft
goat cheese

14 ounces mixed-color
heirloom tomatoes

scant ¾ cup pitted
black olives

a few sprigs of thyme

sea salt flakes
coarse black pepper
extra virgin olive oil

Preheat the oven to 400°F.

Unroll the pastry onto a baking sheet, and with a sharp knife score a ⅜-inch margin around the edge of the pastry—don't cut all the way through, but use enough pressure so that the score line is visible.

Crumble the goat cheese over the pastry, keeping it within the margin. Slice the tomatoes fairly finely—if you don't have a really sharp chef's knife, a serrated knife is always a good option. Arrange the tomato slices, as higgledy-piggledy as possible, on top of the goat cheese, and sprinkle over a pinch of salt and pepper. Roughly chop the olives, and scatter them over the top of the tomatoes along with the thyme.

Bake the tart for 25 to 35 minutes, or until the pastry has puffed up around the tomatoes, and is a light golden brown. Drizzle over a little extra virgin olive oil and serve.

Variation
Thyme is a personal favorite, but sprigs of fresh oregano are just as beautiful. Tarragon or rosemary are very interesting, but not to everyone's taste—the choice is yours.

Pistachio and Artichoke Panzanella

To hell with low-carb salads, this Tuscan bread salad is where the beauty and flavor lies. Other than its beautiful flavor—a combination that I first tried in Napa, California—I just love how the toasted chunks of bread clatter as they are poured into the bowl; it's a successfully inviting sound.

SERVES
4

Cut the bread into roughly ¾-inch cubes. Heat a dry skillet over medium-high heat, and once it is hot, add the bread and toast for a few minutes. The bread cubes need to be crispy and slightly charred, but certainly not burnt. Put the toasted bread into a mixing bowl.

Add the pistachio kernels to the pan, and toss them around for a few minutes, until they smell quite strongly, but don't let them color. Add the toasted pistachios to the bowl with the bread cubes.

Drain the artichokes, discarding the liquid, and blot them dry with some kitchen towels. Chop the artichokes in half, then fry them for just a minute or two to add color, before adding to the bowl.

Finely chop most of the parsley—though do save some whole leaves for finishing—and add to the bowl. Toss everything together until well mixed, then transfer to a large serving plate.

To finish, drizzle the balsamic vinegar over the salad along with about 1 tablespoon olive oil. Scatter the reserved parsley leaves on top. Add a pinch of salt and pepper, and your work is done.

7 ounces stale ciabatta or baguette

1 cup pistachio kernels

8½ ounces drained artichoke hearts (from a 14-ounce jar or can)

Small handful of flat-leaf parsley

2 tablespoons balsamic vinegar

sea salt flakes
coarse black pepper
olive oil

Mushroom and Sage Gnocchi

SERVES
2 to 4

Once of my favorite midweek treats is a bowlful of gorgeously golden gnocchi nuggets. I have dabbled in making my own gnocchi—I love sweet potato and pumpkin varieties—but the package version is such a handy weapon in the kitchen armory, offering almost instant gratification. Ordinarily you boil the gnocchi, similar to pasta, but when fried in butter, it becomes crispy on the outside and tender in the middle. To retain that crispness, I don't want the sauce here to be so thin that it makes the gnocchi soggy; it should be intensely flavored, and thick enough to just coat everything.

---

2 banana shallots

10½ ounces mixed mushrooms

---

8 sage leaves

---

scant ½ cup dry white wine

---

14 ounces gnocchi

---

1 stick butter
sea salt flakes
coarse black pepper
olive oil

Finely chop the shallots and add them, with ½ stick of the butter, to a large skillet set over medium heat. Add a pinch of salt, and reduce the heat to medium-low, frying the shallots until softened—a good 15 minutes should do it. Give the pan a stir every once in a while to prevent the shallots from burning.

Meanwhile, slice the mushrooms thinly and roughly chop half of the sage. When the shallots are softened, increase the heat to high, and throw in the mushrooms. Stir-fry them for a couple of minutes, until they start to soften, then add the chopped sage, and pour in the wine. Allow the wine to bubble and reduce so it coats the mushrooms, but isn't really wet enough to be a sauce. Check the seasoning—you will probably need to add pepper and a touch more salt—then remove from the pan.

Clean the pan and return it to medium heat, then add the remaining ½ stick butter. Once the butter melts, add the gnocchi and fry, without stirring or tossing, for 2 to 3 minutes, until golden brown. Then toss about in the pan, and fry for a few minutes more. The gnocchi should be slightly crispy, so they clatter quietly and invitingly when moved. Return the mushrooms to the pan and stir to coat the gnocchi.

To garnish, heat at least 3 tablespoons oil in a small saucepan and allow it to get hot, then add the remaining 4 sage leaves, frying them for just a minute, maybe less, until crispy. Remove from the pan and blot on kitchen towels. Serve generous, heaping platefuls of the gnocchi with a crispy sage leaf or two.

Roasted Green Beans and Chickpeas with Tamarind

Generally, when vegetables are roasted they become sweeter: the natural sugars caramelize and water evaporates, so the flavor is far more concentrated. That's precisely what happens with the beans here, so the natural counterpart would be something tangy and sour. Tamarind is mouth-puckering, and I like it.

SERVES
1 to 2

Preheat the oven to 425°F.

Drain the chickpeas and put into a large roasting pan. Trim the beans and put on top of the chickpeas with 1 teaspoon pepper, 1 tablespoon oil and 2 tablespoons of the fish sauce, then toss everything together to coat. Roast for 25 to 30 minutes, until the beans have shriveled and the chickpeas look dry.

Put the roasted beans and chickpeas into a mixing bowl, add the tamarind paste with the remaining fish sauce, and toss to coat. Roughly chop the cilantro, and scatter over the top before serving.

Leftover ingredient
Use the leftover tamarind paste in my Curried Romanesco and Tamarind Soup on page 36.

1 (15-ounce) can chickpeas

10 ounces fine green beans

4 tablespoons fish sauce

4 teaspoons tamarind paste

small handful of fresh cilantro

coarse black pepper
olive oil

Lime and Thyme Carrots with Salmon Fillets

SERVES
4

My mother always roasts her carrots in lime juice and thyme, and they are incomparably good. She does that old-fashioned thing of cutting the carrots into angled shards, but I've evolved that, and now use baby carrots. I prefer to use the ones with a little bit of stalk intact, but feel free to chop that off if you prefer. When it comes to choosing the juiciest limes, I always give them a good squeeze—they shouldn't be rock solid, but rather should yield a little.

14 ounces baby carrots

4 banana shallots

juice of 2 limes

4 sprigs of thyme

4 salmon fillets

sea salt flakes
coarse black pepper

Preheat the oven to 350°F.

Place the carrots in a large roasting pan. Peel the shallots and slice them in half lengthwise, and add to the pan along with the lime juice, thyme, and 1 teaspoon each of salt and pepper. Cover with foil and roast for 1 hour.

While the carrots roast, season the salmon fillets with a pinch of salt and pepper. After the carrots have cooked for 1 hour in the oven, remove the foil and place the salmon fillets into the roasting pan. Return to the oven for 12 to 15 minutes, until the salmon is cooked through.

Shrimp, Mango, and Peanut Noodle Salad

SERVES
2 to 4

Store-bought, ready-cooked jumbo shrimp are such handy little creatures to have in the fridge. Here, with just a few minor preparatory movements, you have a wholesome salad in very little time.

First, rehydrate the noodles: put them into a heatproof bowl, and pour over enough boiling water to submerge them entirely. Leave them to soak for 3 minutes, until soft, then drain, and allow to cool to room temperature.

Peel and pit the mango—the best way is to slice off each cheek, then peel it carefully with a potato peeler. Slice the mango flesh into long, thin slices.

Arrange the noodles on a large plate, and top with the shrimp and mango slices. Drizzle over the chili sauce, then roughly chop the peanuts and scatter them over the top. Season if you feel as though it needs it—I personally like a pinch of pepper on this.

5½ ounces thin vermicelli rice noodles

1 medium mango

10½ ounces cooked jumbo shrimp

3 tablespoons hot sweet chili dipping sauce

scant ½ cup salted peanuts

coarse black pepper (optional)

Puttanesca-style Monkfish Stew

SERVES
4

Puttanesca sauce isn't for those with a delicate palate; it is hot, fiery, and gutsy. It relies entirely on the brash flavors of salt, chiles, and garlic. Traditionally the sauce is made with black olives and salted anchovies. Not wanting to lose either of those vital components, I've opted for anchovy-stuffed green olives—they seem to be much more easy to come by than black, but if you do see anchovy-stuffed black olives, use those.

2 fat red chiles

3½ ounces jarred
anchovy-stuffed
green olives

5 garlic cloves

14 ounces canned
chopped tomatoes

8 (5-ounce)
monkfish fillets

sea salt flakes
coarse black pepper
olive oil

Roughly chop the chiles—I don't bother to seed them—half of the olives, and all of the garlic, then add to a mortar and pestle, and grind to a rough paste with 1 teaspoon each of salt and pepper. You could also pulse this in a small food processor, if you prefer.

In a deep-sided skillet or Dutch oven—one you have a lid for—heat 3 tablespoons of olive oil over high heat, and once it is hot, add the paste. Stir the paste constantly for a good minute until it has a strong aroma—don't let it stick to and burn on the pan. Once the paste is fragrant, add the tomatoes, and bring to a bubble. Reduce to a simmer, and lay the monkfish fillets on top. Chop the remaining olives, and scatter them over the fish, then pop on a lid, and simmer gently for 10 minutes, or until the fish is almost completely cooked through and tender.

Remove from the heat, leaving the lid on, and allow to steam for a few minutes before serving.

Variation
Monkfish works well because it is so meaty, and can easily hold its own against that bold sauce. If you need to use a different fish, make sure you choose a meaty white one—hake, pollock, or cod would be ideal.

Dilly Devilish Garlic Shrimp

SERVES
2

When you eat with your hands (which you absolutely must here), there's something gratifying about a spicy oiliness that coats your fingers and face. And if eaten in a romantic setting, the stickiness helps to break down that initial awkwardness; there's nothing sexier than someone who both loves and lives to eat.

---

3 fat red chiles

---

6 large garlic cloves

---

18 ounces raw jumbo
shrimp, shells on

¼ cup vodka

Small handful of dill

---

olive oil
sea salt flakes
coarse black pepper

Finely slice the chiles—I don't bother to seed—and garlic, and keep them separate. Heat ⅓ cup olive oil in a skillet over medium-high heat, and once it is hot, add just the chiles, and stir-fry for about 30 seconds to infuse the oil. Add the shrimp with the garlic, and fry for about 1 minute. Flip the shrimp over, and add the vodka to the pan, along with a pinch of salt and pepper. Fry for an additional minute—the ghostly gray of the shrimp should become a warm, pinkish coral.

Roughly chop the dill, and scatter it over the shrimp. You could serve this in the pan, though the shrimp may continue to cook in the residual heat, and become a little tough, so it's probably best to tip them out onto a serving plate.

Lemongrass and Chile Clam Broth

SERVES
2 to 4

When I'm feeling a little under the weather, or simply downtrodden, I'll crave a bowlful of broth spiced with lemongrass, chile, and cilantro. Recently I was given some clams, and decided to merge my cold-curing broth—which was already made, and in the fridge—with my prize. It works beautifully, and is such a quick dish to rustle up.

2¼ pounds clams

3 lemongrass stalks

4 fat red chiles

Small handful of
fresh cilantro

4½ cups good-quality
chicken stock

½ stick unsalted butter
coarse black pepper
sea salt flakes (optional)

Put the clams into a colander and rinse under cold running water for a minute. Give the clams a shake, and discard any that don't close when tapped on the worktop.

With the back of a knife, bash the lemongrass stalks repeatedly to release all the flavorful oils, and then slice them in half. Slice each half into four, lengthwise, to give thin shards of lemongrass. Slice the chiles in half lengthwise—you can remove the stalk if you wish, but I don't bother. Separate the leaves from the cilantro stalks, placing them in a bowl to one side. Roughly chop the cilantro stalks, and have them handy with the lemongrass and chile.

In a heavy-bottomed Dutch oven or large saucepan—one you have a lid for—heat the butter over high heat, and once the butter melts, throw in the lemongrass, chile, and chopped cilantro stalks. Stir-fry for just 1 minute, then add the stock. Bring to a boil, reduce to a gentle simmer, and pop on the lid. Cook for 20 minutes to infuse the stock with all of the glorious aromatics. Test the seasoning, adding plenty of pepper, and salt if necessary.

Return the pan to a boil, and add the clams. Put on the lid and cook for a final 5 minutes, then remove from the heat. Scatter over the reserved cilantro leaves and serve. Don't eat any clams that don't open during the cooking process.

Tahini and Honey Chicken and Paprika Potatoes

In Paris, on Rue Mouffetard, there is a small stand from which chicken and potatoes are sold. The chicken is slowly cooked on a rotisserie, and the fat weeps down onto the potatoes, basting them as they cook. Served in a white foil bag, it makes for the ultimate Parisian lunch, devoured from a park bench.

That experience inspired this dish in a way, only here I've added some of my favorite Middle Eastern flavors. The mix of tahini and honey is really superb, and crisps up beautifully on the chicken.

SERVES
4

⅔ cup tahini

4½ tablespoons clear honey

8 chicken drumsticks

About 24 small new potatoes

1 tablespoon paprika

sea salt flakes
coarse black pepper
olive or canola oil

Preheat the oven to 400°F.

In a large bowl, mix together the tahini and honey with 1 teaspoon each of salt and pepper. Remove the skin from the chicken drumsticks, and slash each one three times. Add the drumsticks to the marinade and coat them well. Refrigerate until you are ready to roast.

Slice the potatoes in half, though leave any particularly tiny ones whole, and transfer to a large roasting pan. Add 1 tablespoon olive oil, a pinch of salt and pepper, and the paprika, toss together until the potatoes are well coated, and roast for 20 minutes.

After this time, lay the drumsticks on top of the potatoes, and roast for an additional 25 to 30 minutes, until the chicken is cooked through, and the marinade is crispy.

Roasted Sausage and Apple with Sauerkraut

A midweek sausage supper is reassuringly simple, and even better, it doesn't skimp on flavor or the general feeling of being satisfied. The best-quality sausages are always a must: I'd opt for the supermarket's best own brand or those from an excellent butcher. And, of course, you can quite easily, and absolutely should, customize this dish with different flavors of sausage—a fiery, chile-flecked sausage would do just the trick for me.

SERVES
2 to 4

Preheat the oven to 400°F.

Put the sausages into a roasting pan and drizzle with a little olive oil. Cut the apples into quarters—I don't bother to core or peel them. Slice the onion in half through the root, leaving the root intact, and peel it. Cut it into eight wedges and arrange these, with the apples, in the roasting pan. Top with the thyme sprigs, and season with a pinch of salt and pepper.

Roast for 30 to 40 minutes, until the sausages are bronzed, and the apples and onion are quite softened. You can turn the sausages midway through, if you prefer a more even coloring; though I'm not particularly concerned. Scatter over the sauerkraut just before serving.

8 good-quality
link sausages

2 Granny Smith apples

1 large onion

A few sprigs of thyme

2 tablespoons
sauerkraut

olive oil
sea salt flakes
coarse black pepper

Leftover ingredient
The sauerkraut will keep for a while in the fridge. It's gorgeous in ham sandwiches, stirred into soups, scattered over pizzas or stews. It brings its flavor-boosting qualities to any dish, really, but it's delicious in its own right, too.

Harissa Minute Steak Kebabs

SERVES
4

Harissa is one of the things I always have in the cupboard in abundant supply. It is warming and spicy, yet ever so slightly tangy, and goes perfectly with pretty much anything—I've been known to toss together flaked mackerel with harissa and pasta as a lazy, last-minute lunch. I particularly love the deep red-pepper paste here on the minute steaks: because the steaks are so thin, you can rest assured that with every bite, you'll get oodles of spicy flavor.

21 ounces minute steaks

4½ ounces harissa paste

4 flatbreads

4 tablespoons hummus (I like red pepper hummus here)

Jar of green pickled jalapeño peppers

sea salt flakes
coarse black pepper
olive oil

Mix together the steaks, harissa, and a pinch of salt and pepper in a mixing bowl. Cover with plastic wrap, and allow to marinate at room temperature for 30 minutes. You could even do this in the morning before you head out, and just refrigerate until needed.

Place a skillet over medium–high heat, and once it is hot, fry the steaks for about 45 seconds per side. Remove the steaks from the heat and onto a plate, covering them with foil.

Warm the flatbreads in the pan for just a few seconds on each side, then spread each with hummus. Slice the minute steaks into small strips and scatter over the hummus, then add the jalapeño peppers—as many as folk may fancy. Be sure to drizzle any steak juices left on the plate over the top before serving.

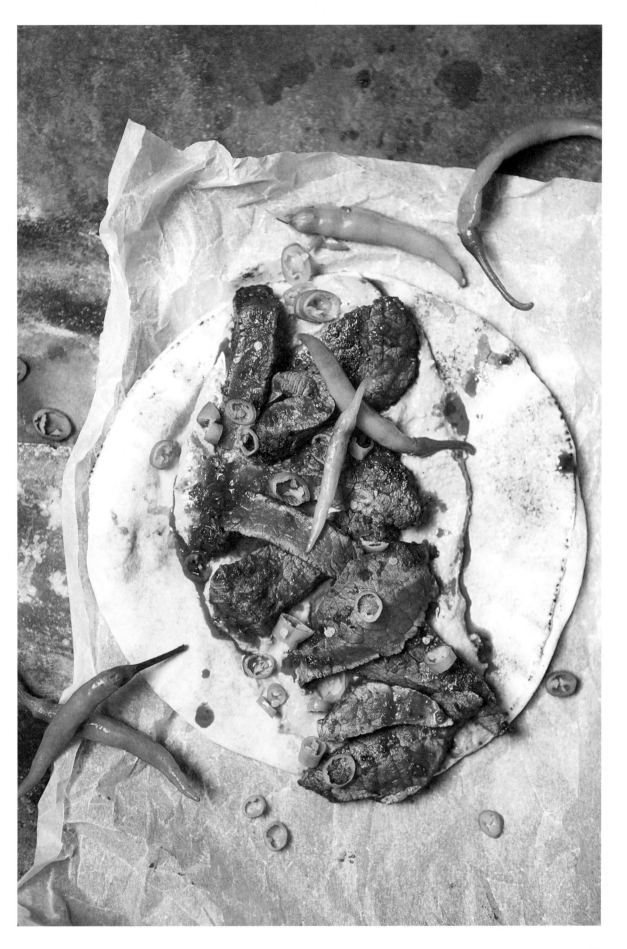

Orange and Sumac Flat Iron Steak with Eggplant and Artichoke

SERVES
4

Although steak, French fries, and Béarnaise sauce is a difficult combination to compete with, this is a gorgeous alternative recipe for steak. The orange not only offers a refreshing tang, but its acidity helps to tenderize the steaks, too. Sumac is a deep red spice with a sharp, citrus flavor, and is absolutely gorgeous with most meats.

The steaks are turned frequently during frying, and that's because with flat iron, as with skirt and flank, the fibrous steak is very easily overcooked and can become tough. This method ensures an even, gentle cooking.

2 oranges

2 tablespoons sumac

4 (5-ounce) flat iron steaks

2 eggplants

14 ounces (ish) jar or can artichoke hearts

olive or canola oil
sea salt flakes
coarse black pepper

To make the marinade, simply combine the zest and juice of one of the oranges with half of the sumac and 1 tablespoon oil. Rub this into the steaks, wrap them in plastic wrap, and leave to marinate at room temperature for 1 hour.

Season the steaks with salt and pepper, then fry each in a hot skillet for 6 minutes, turning them every minute. If you prefer the steaks a little less rare, fry as above for 8 minutes. After this time, wrap the steaks in foil, and allow to rest for a good 10 minutes.

Dice the eggplants into 1-inch chunks, and halve the artichoke hearts. Drench the eggplants in 2 tablespoons oil and a good pinch of salt and pepper. Heat a skillet over high heat, and once it is hot, add the eggplant and stir-fry for about 5 minutes, until slightly colored. Drain the artichokes, and fry them for 1 minute. Place onto plates. Peel and slice the remaining orange, and add to the plates, then sprinkle over the remaining sumac.

Slice the steaks into thin strips—do this against the grain of the meat to ensure you get tender pieces—and set on top of the eggplant and artichoke salad. Pour any juices from the foil over the top and serve.

WORTH-THE-WAIT PLATES

SLOW COOKED

There's a smug reassurance in knowing you've got something slowly cooking at home, piping hot and ready for when you return. Whether you're stressed out at work or traipsing around in the cold, when your mind flicks back to that warm stew, all stresses seem trivial—if only for a split second. And on returning to the kitchen, you're greeted with the ravishing aroma of whatever has been quietly and confidently doing its thing all day. The ultimate welcome home.

I suppose, for that reason, this could be a sub-chapter within the comfort food part of this book: there's no denying that slow-cooked meals have a cockle-warming cosiness to them. But equally, some of these recipes could have slotted into the everyday plates chapter, because cooking like this requires very little attention or effort. It's just a matter of getting the ingredients prepared, then letting them cook away. That's not to say that slow cooking involves no thought whatsoever; it absolutely does. It's important to think about how the meat will cook: if the particular cut is diced too small it leaves a greater surface area to meat ratio, so there's a risk of the meat drying out all too quickly. But there's little need to worry about all that here because in these recipes I've done the working out for you.

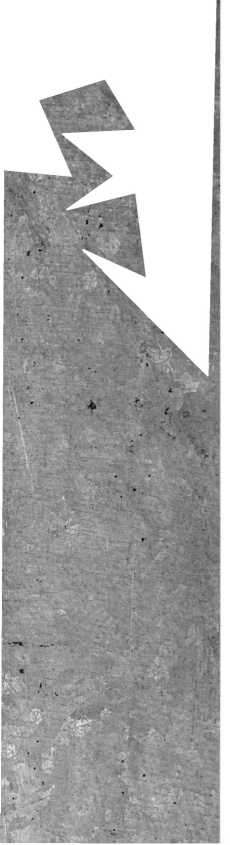

So these recipes are worthy, I feel, of a chapter of their very own. This is a slow-cooked chapter, but it isn't a slow cooker chapter; I do all of my slow cooking in the oven. Environmentalists may harp, but it's not a decision I've made without due consideration. If the main reason for buying a slow cooker is to reduce electricity consumption, that is fair enough—slow cookers use far less energy than a domestic electric oven. In my constant pursuit of flavor, though, I find that slow cookers never seem to do the job quite properly. The results, for me, are often too watery or insipid; the oven seems to force the flavors to merge and mingle. But you might think my fear is ill-founded, so feel free to use whichever method suits you best; just make sure that if you do use a slow cooker, follow the manufacturer's instructions with my method in mind.

That being said, whichever you choose, it's impossible for me to be too prescriptive about timings. As soon as the meat flakes apart when pronged with a fork, take it away from its heat source. This inaccuracy is down to so many variables: while modern ovens are reasonably reliable, there could still be discrepancy. The pot in which the food is cooked has an unbelievable impact: too thin a material, and the dish could quickly overheat. To avoid doubt, for any recipes that are cooked in a "Dutch oven" or "heavy-bottomed saucepan," I use a Le Creuset 9½-inch cast-iron dutch oven.

One of the best things about slow cooking is how the fatty, collagen-rich meats can be cooked until they're mouthwateringly tender—fat is life's lubrication as far as I'm concerned. If, for some reason (I'll withhold judgement here), you want to reduce the amount of fat in the dish, I'd recommend you leave it overnight in the fridge before serving the next day. That way, the fat will solidify at the surface and you can easily scoop it off. I don't bother to remove the fat, but I do believe that chilling the food overnight improves the flavor and the texture of the meat anyway, so it's a practice I always undertake.

Four-hour Tomato Pasta Sauce

SERVES
4

You might think life is too short to peel tomatoes, and then slowly cook them down into a sauce. And admittedly (I'm not trying to put you off, I promise) you don't get much yield for the amount of tomatoes you buy. But as soon as you taste this sauce, you are reassured that it was all totally worthwhile. You may believe you've already had the best pasta sauce possible, but so often it will, in fact, have been too acidic and watery— the result of using canned tomatoes. Fresh plum tomatoes are best in a sauce like this, as they are far fleshier than regular salad tomatoes.

3½ pounds fresh
plum tomatoes

---

1 large red onion

---

3 garlic cloves

½ cup Italian red wine
(Malbec if available)

---

14 ounces dried pasta
(linguine or tagliolini)

---

scant 3 tablespoons
unsalted butter
sea salt flakes
coarse black pepper

Preheat the oven to 325°F.

To peel the tomatoes, place them in a large heatproof mixing bowl—I do this in two batches—then cover them with boiling water. Leave the tomatoes for a minute or two, then drain off the water and plunge them into cold water. Once they are cool enough to handle, remove the skin; it should hopefully slip right off, but if it doesn't, just pull it carefully. Chop the tomatoes roughly, then set aside.

In a Dutch oven or heavy-bottomed saucepan—one you have a lid for—melt the butter over medium heat. Finely chop the onion, and add to the melted butter with a pinch of salt, and once it starts to sizzle, reduce the heat to low, and cook down, stirring frequently, for 20 minutes until mushy, but reasonably uncolored. Peel the garlic, and throw the whole cloves into the pan along with the tomatoes and a pinch of pepper. Add the wine, and bring to a boil, then cover with a lid, and cook for 3½ to 4 hours. Do check it after 3 hours, and if it's looking a little dry, add a splash of water.

Once the sauce is ready, check the seasoning, and add more salt and pepper if required—I like a lot of pepper here, at least 1 teaspoon, but the choice is yours. Cook the pasta according to the package instructions, but make sure you put a very generous pinch of salt into the cooking water before adding the pasta.

To serve, stir the pasta through the sauce to coat each strand, then pile, casually, onto plates.

Preserved Lemon and Cider Pork with Couscous

SERVES
4 to 6

The idea of slow cooking may conjure up images of wintry stews and warming hunks of braised meats, but this method can be a summery pursuit, too. I suppose it's all down to what you throw into the pot. The pear cider here is crisp and sweet, and so it marries well with the pork. The preserved lemon gives a little extra sharpness, which perfectly complements the otherwise bland couscous.

3½ pounds
shoulder of pork

5¼ cups hard pear
(or apple) cider

---

6 preserved lemons

---

8 sprigs of thyme, plus
extra for the couscous

2⅓ cups couscous

Preheat the oven to 325°F. If it hasn't already been done, (and you are lucky enough to have some), remove the crackling skin and fat from the pork, and place it onto a baking sheet. Deeply score a few times, rub a little salt into both sides, then set aside.

Heat a heavy-bottomed saucepan or dutch oven over high heat, and add 1 tablespoon oil. Once the oil shimmers, add the pork shoulder to the pan, and sear for about 3 minutes, turning occasionally to ensure all of the flesh is seared. Add the cider, 4 of the whole preserved lemons, the thyme sprigs, and a pinch of salt and pepper. Bring to a boil, then cover with a lid, and put into the oven with the pan of crackling—you'll probably need to use two shelves. Allow to cook slowly for about 4 hours, until the crackling is incredibly crisp, and the pork meat is falling apart.

After this time, take everything out of the oven. Remove the crackling from the pan, and allow to cool and crisp on a plate. Remove the pork from the pan, and put it onto a plate, covering it with foil.

Put the couscous into a heatproof bowl and place the pan of cooking liquor over high heat, and bring to a boil. Once it is boiling, pour enough of the liquid over the couscous to cover by ¾ inch—you may need to top up with boiling water. Cover the bowl with a plate or plastic wrap, and leave to soak for 10 minutes or so. Fluff up the couscous with a fork, and season to taste, adding a small handful of chopped thyme leaves, and the remaining preserved lemons, roughly chopped. Shred the pork, and serve it on a mound of couscous, topped with some crispy pieces of crackling.

Grapefruit Marmalade Pork Belly with Caramelized Red Cabbage

I adore pork belly; it's one of my favorite cuts of pork. But because it is fatty, it needs to be cooked fairly slowly, and it should be served with something quite sharp to cut through it all.

SERVES
4

The day before cooking, cut the pork belly in half and place it in a resealable food bag. In a mixing bowl, dissolve 4 tablespoons salt in 4½ cups of the water, then stir in 1 tablespoon pepper, pour it all into the bag with the pork, and seal. Refrigerate overnight, or for at least 8 hours.

Preheat the oven to 475°F. Place the pork slices, out of their brine, skin-side up in a deep roasting dish and roast, uncovered, for just 30 minutes.

Meanwhile, mix together the remaining water and the marmalade with ½ teaspoon salt and 1 teaspoon pepper.

Take the pork from the oven, reduce the temperature to 325°F, then pour the marmalade mixture over the pork slices and cover the roasting dish with foil. Return the pork to the oven and cook for an additional 2 hours, until the meat is incredibly tender. Increase the heat of the oven to 475°F and remove the foil. Cook for a final 10 to 15 minutes. Remove from the oven to rest.

Meanwhile, thinly shred the cabbage. Heat the butter in a skillet over high heat, then add the cabbage, and turn the heat down to medium-high. Stir-fry for 5 minutes, then add the sugar and vinegar, and cook, over low heat, for 15 minutes until soft and caramelized.

Remove the pork from the cooking juices, and cut each piece in half. Skim the excess fat from the cooking juices, and discard, then serve the cabbage with the pork and a drizzle of the juices.

3½ pound piece of boneless and rindless pork belly

---

6 tablespoons grapefruit marmalade

---

1 small red cabbage

---

2 tablespoons light brown sugar

---

2 tablespoons cider vinegar

---

sea salt flakes
coarse black pepper
5¼ cups water
2 tablespoons unsalted butter

Pork Osso Buco with Turnips, Anise, and Orange

SERVES
4

The Italian "osso buco" just means "bone with a hole" (which refers to the cross-cut of the shank bone), but has become the name for the classic Milanese dish of veal shanks, wine and vegetables. I stumbled across pork hock osso buco in a local supermarket and I yelped with excitement.

Somehow it is the turnips that make this dish so successful. The other flavors are vital, too, of course—I wouldn't dream of discounting the exotic combination of star anise and shaoxing wine—but that familiar pepperiness of the turnips is what I love so much about this. It's like a reassuring phone call home during a long-distance vacation.

Preheat the oven to 350°F.

3½ pounds pork osso buco (about 8 pieces)

10½ ounces turnips

½ cup shaoxing (Chinese rice) wine

4 star anise

2 unwaxed oranges

sea salt flakes
olive oil
coarse black pepper
1¾ cups water

In a large saucepan or flameproof Dutch oven—one you have a lid for—heat 1 tablespoon olive oil over high heat. Season the osso buco pieces with a pinch of salt and pepper, then fry until golden brown and seared—this is best done in batches. While the meat sears (though do toss it about the pan frequently), peel the turnips, and cut into ½-inch dice.

Once all the meat is seared, add the turnips to the pan along with the shaoxing, and allow the liquid to come to a boil, then return the meat to the pan with the star anise, the juice, and thinly pared peel of one of the oranges, and the water. Put on the lid and cook for 2½ hours in the oven—the meat should be so tender that it is starting to fall from the bone.

Remove the pork and turnips with a slotted spoon, then bring the cooking liquor back to a boil on the stove. Boil until reduced by half, then return everything back to the pan to coat. Peel, segment, and roughly chop the remaining orange and add to the stew before serving.

Variation

If you can't for the life of you get hold of osso buco, use an unrolled pork shoulder, trimmed of its fat. In that case, you could cook the crackling as in the recipe on page 98. It would need a longer cooking time—4 hours should do it.

Black Grape Lamb Shanks

When experimenting with this recipe, I was thrilled to discover that the grapes don't mush to nothing, as one might expect. Instead they become plump and satin matte, like unpolished gemstones. The cooking liquor becomes a dark indigo; it too was revealed to squeals of surprise.

The trick with this dish is to reduce the cooking liquid before serving. That process intensifies the flavor and thickens the sauce, so it becomes more of a hearty stew than a dainty broth.

Preheat the oven to 400°F.

Peel and roughly chop the onion and remove the grapes from their stalks.

Sprinkle a generous pinch of salt and pepper over the lamb, and rub it in all over the surface of each shank. Heat 3 tablespoons olive oil in a heavy-bottomed Dutch oven over high heat, and once the oil is hot, add the shanks. Fry on each side for a minute or so, until the skin is golden brown. Add the grapes, onion, rosemary, and water to the pan. Bring the liquid to a boil, and then cover everything with a disc of parchment paper before clamping on a lid— if you don't have a lid, seal well with foil. Put into the oven, and cook for 2 hours.

After this time, remove the shanks and some (about half) of the grapes and onions from the liquid, and put onto a plate, covering with foil. Bring the liquid to a boil on the stove, and reduce by about a half—you want it to be reasonably thick. Drain the beans, add those to the pan, and cook to warm them through. Check the seasoning, adding a little more salt and pepper if required, and serve the lamb shanks on top of that purple, bean-studded stew.

SERVES
4

1 large onion

14 ounces black grapes

4 lamb shanks

4 sprigs of rosemary

1 (15-ounce) can black beans

sea salt flakes
coarse black pepper
olive oil
1¾ cups water

Five-hour Lamb with Potato Gratin

SERVES
6 to 8

A slow-roasted leg of lamb will always earn you a few gasps of surprise from whoever witnesses its unveiling. The flavor here not only comes from that slow-cooking process, but also from the gutsy marinade of anchovies, garlic, and mint; every single flake of lamb is gorgeous. The potatoes, sitting snugly under the lamb, catch all of the meat's juices as it roasts, and so become incredibly tender.

3½ ounces jarred
anchovies in olive oil

8 garlic cloves

1 tablespoon
mint sauce

4½ pounds
leg of lamb

6 medium russet or
Yukon gold potatoes

sea salt flakes
coarse black pepper

For the marinade, blitz the anchovies and the oil they came in, with the peeled garlic cloves and the mint sauce to a smooth paste in a food processor. If you don't have a food processor, you could make the paste using a sharp knife and bold ambition. Stir in 1 teaspoon each of salt and pepper.

With a sharp knife, stab the lamb leg repeatedly all over—you need as many deep cuts as possible, without completely massacring the meat. Spread the paste over the entire surface of the meat, working it well into the cuts. Refrigerate for an hour, or until required.

Preheat the oven to 325°F. Remove the lamb from the fridge 1 hour before it goes into the oven, to bring it up to room temperature.

Slice the unpeeled potatoes as finely as possible—I use a mandoline—and arrange them in layers in a deep-sided roasting dish, seasoning with a very small pinch of salt and pepper every couple of layers. Place the lamb on top of the potato slices. Cover with a couple of sheets of foil, ensuring you seal it extremely well. Roast for 4½ hours.

Remove the dish from the oven, and increase the heat to 425°F. Remove the foil, and baste the lamb with some of the juices from the roasting dish. Put everything back into the oven for an additional 30 minutes. Remove the lamb from the oven, transfer it to a plate, cover it with foil and leave to rest. Return the potatoes to the oven for a final 25 to 30 minutes, until slightly crispy around the edges.

Lamb, Cherry, and Yellow Split Pea Tagine

SERVES
4

As with most slow-cooked stews, the meat is so gently braised, that when cooked, it just flakes into tender pieces. The flavor combination here is somewhat of a cross-cultural mix: the ras el hanout is a North African spice blend (an exotic mixture of cardamom, cumin, cinnamon, rose, and much more), while the cherry and lamb pairing is more Middle Eastern in its inspiration.

2¼ pounds diced
lamb leg

---

2 tablespoons *ras
el hanout* spice
blend, plus extra
for sprinkling

---

heaping 1⅓ cups
yellow split peas

1½ cups dried
sour cherries

---

1 unwaxed lemon

---

olive oil
sea salt flakes
coarse black pepper
4½ cups water

Preheat the oven to 325°F.

In a large heavy-bottomed saucepan or Dutch oven—one you have a lid for—heat 1 tablespoon olive oil over high heat. Once the oil is hot, add the pieces of lamb—it's probably best to do this in two batches—and fry until browned all over. Add the *ras el hanout* with a generous pinch of salt and pepper, and stir to coat the pieces of lamb. Add the split peas and cherries, stirring to coat them in the spices, then add the water.

Peel the zest from the lemon with a potato peeler—try to avoid getting too much white pith on the strips—and add the peel to the pan. Bring the pan to a boil, then cover with a lid or foil, and cook in the oven for 3½ to 4 hours—the lamb should be exceedingly tender, and the peas cooked through. Do check the tagine after 2 hours, and add a splash of water if it looks dry.

Serve in bowls, with a squeeze of lemon juice, and a sprinkle of *ras el hanout*.

Variation

If you can't find the yellow split peas, just use green. Failing that, split lentils would be lovely, too. If the cherries are difficult to come by, dried cranberries would be a slightly more sour option, or use dried blueberries.

Spiced Wine Brisket with Roasted Cauliflower

When I think of slow cooking, my mouth waters at the image of a beef brisket submerged in liquid and gently braised. The spiced wine here is first used for flavor—those subtle spices permeate into the meat—but also because its slightly acidic nature helps to break down the collagen in the meat, so you end up with something incredibly tender and tasty.

SERVES
4 to 6

Preheat the oven to 250°F.

Finely slice the onions and add to a large Dutch oven— one you have a lid for. Add the butter and a pinch of salt, and cook over medium heat until the onions start to sizzle. Reduce the heat to low, and cook slowly, stirring occasionally, for 30 minutes, or until the onions are very mushy and caramelized. Remove the onions from the pan and increase the heat to high. Add the beef and sear for about a minute on each side.

Pour the wine over the meat, and return the onions to the pan along with 1 teaspoon pepper. Bring to a boil, cover with a lid, and slow-cook in the oven for 6 to 8 hours. You want the meat to be extremely tender; if you pull at a corner, it should flake away with little resistance.

Meanwhile, chop the cauliflower into medium-sized florets, and chop the stalk into similar-sized pieces. Arrange in a roasting pan, drizzle with 2 tablespoons olive oil, and add a pinch of salt and pepper. Mince the garlic, and add to the pan, then toss everything together.

Once the meat is cooked, remove it from the oven, and let rest, covered, in the pan. Increase the oven temperature to 400°F. Roast the cauliflower for 35 to 40 minutes, tossing it every 15 minutes, until slightly charred and tender.

Remove the meat from the cooking liquor, and cover with foil. Boil the cooking liquor, uncovered, until reduced by half. Season to taste, then serve—I shred the meat, but you can just serve it in hearty slices, if you prefer.

3 red onions

3¼ pounds unrolled beef brisket

one (750ml) bottle spiced wine

1 large head of cauliflower

2 garlic cloves

½ stick unsalted butter
sea salt flakes
coarse black pepper
olive oil

Beef Cheek in Port with Parsnip Mash

SERVES
4 to 6

Beef cheek is one of my favorite slow-cook cuts of beef. Because the cut is rich in collagen, it makes for such a succulent stew. Sadly, its availability has declined in recent years, but a good butcher will have some in, and if they don't, they'll happily order it for you.

The slow cooking and the reduction of the cooking liquor make this into a very rich stew, but with the addition of the vinegar-soaked onions, it's perfectly balanced.

3¼ pounds
beef cheek

---

2 medium red onions

---

5 teaspoons
sherry vinegar

---

2 cups ruby port

2¾ pounds parsnips

---

sea salt flakes
olive oil
coarse black pepper
scant ⅔ cup unsalted butter

Preheat the oven to 325°F.

Slice each beef cheek into about 6 pieces and toss them with a pinch of salt. Peel and halve the onions and save one half for later. Slice the remaining three halves as finely as possible, and put into a bowl to one side until required.

Heat 2 tablespoons oil over high heat in a heavy-bottomed saucepan or flameproof Dutch oven—one you have a lid for. When the oil is hot, add the beef cheek, and fry for a few minutes until deeply colored—you'll need to do this in two or three batches, otherwise the meat won't brown. Once the meat is seared, put it onto a plate and set aside.

Add another tablespoon of oil to the pan, along with the larger quantity of onions. Turn the heat down to medium–low, and add 1 teaspoon of the vinegar, and a pinch of salt. Fry the onions slowly, stirring frequently, for about 20 minutes, or until soft but not mushy.

Return the beef cheek to the pan with 2 teaspoons pepper and all but 2 tablespoons of the port. Bring the port to a boil, then cover, and slow-cook in the oven for 3½ to 4 hours, or until the meat is beautifully tender—it should flake apart, but it should not be dry. Do keep an eye on the pan and check it after 2 hours: if it looks too dry, add a glug of water, though if your pan is any good, it won't let too much moisture escape. And it's worth giving it a stir halfway through.

Slice the remaining onion half as finely as possible, put it into a small bowl with the remaining vinegar and a pinch of salt, and set aside.

For the parsnip mash, peel the parsnips and cut them into even-sized chunks, pop them into a pan, and cover with water. Bring to a boil, and cook for 10 to 15 minutes, or until a knife pierces the flesh easily, but they remain intact. Drain the water, and return the parsnips to the pan, off the heat, with the butter and a pinch of salt and pepper. When the butter starts to melt, mash the parsnips roughly.

When the meat is cooked, remove the beef cheek from the pan with a slotted spoon, put it into a bowl, and cover with foil to rest. Bring the cooking liquor to a boil over high heat until reduced by a quarter, then stir in the remaining 2 tablespoons of port. Check the seasoning, adding more salt and pepper if necessary.

Serve a mound of parsnip mash topped with the beef cheek, a generous drizzle of the intense port sauce, and the vinegar-soaked onion slices.

Variation
Red wine or cider vinegar would be acceptable alternatives to sherry vinegar.

POSH PLATES

IMPRESSIVE DISHES

I've never seen the value in meddling with ingredients so severely that they no longer resemble food. I find it exhausting; I'd much rather eat something bland-looking and totally addictive than something that looks spectacular, but has been prodded and poked until it tastes of absolutely nothing. I've already expressed a deep-rooted disdain for "molecular gastronomy" in this book (mocking quotation marks necessary here), but it bears repeating: that is not my idea of food. As a science or art form, yes, it can be impressive, but frankly, I'd much rather do a tour of the Tate Modern Museum while chowing down on a hotdog bought from a nearby vendor.

For me, all food has the inherent ability to evoke admiration. There are times in everyone's life when they want to do something a little bit special with food; we all long to be appreciated or loved. Food is the ultimate conveyer of love, and, lucky for us cooks, it is the perfect tool to ensure that love and admiration are reciprocated.

But as well as having a softer, caring side, I am all too well versed in the art of one-upmanship. Sometimes it's just necessary. I'm not proud of this, you understand, but there have been times when I've wanted to blow little Miss Marvelous and her smorgasbord of dreams out of the water. And I've done just that; while food is mainly about love, it can be the ultimate weapon, too. I didn't poison her poussin or anything; I just put on a superior spread.

With all of that emotional turmoil in mind, and whatever your motive, this chapter should come as welcome reassurance for when you want to impress. That's not to say that the recipes here are sophisticated to the extent that they are impossible to re-create; it's important that the path of love or revenge is as smooth as possible. The dishes simply use slightly different ingredients that you might not expect to include on a day-to-day basis. One or two of these recipes may take a little more time than an everyday plate, but there's no secret or wizardry here; it's all just cooking.

Asparagus and Leeks Braised in Riesling, and Tarragon with Prosciutto

SERVES
2

This is one of those suppers that is reasonably balanced, but brings the smugness of both ease and comfort. The sweet Riesling, once evaporated and thickened, coupled with the gentle anise flavor of the tarragon, transforms the vegetables entirely.

You may notice I don't add any salt here. I just find that the reduced wine has such a startling body to it—and the prosciutto is salty enough—that additional salt would be overkill. But, your palate, your preference.

9 ounces asparagus
spears

6 ounces baby leeks

scant 1 cup
Riesling wine

5 sprigs of tarragon

8 strips of prosciutto

generous ½ stick
unsalted butter
coarse black pepper

Trim the woody ends off the asparagus spears—I hold the root end in one hand, halfway up the stalk with the other, then gently bend it until it snaps. Wherever it breaks tends to be just about right. Rinse both the asparagus and the leeks, and dry completely with a clean kitchen cloth.

In a large, shallow Dutch oven—one you have a lid for—heat half the butter over medium-high heat. Once melted, add the asparagus and leeks, and fry, turning once, for a few minutes until gently colored. I'm not bothered that the butter might burn here; in fact, those nutty qualities will enhance the dish.

When the vegetables are colored, pour in the wine, and throw in the tarragon with a pinch of pepper. Pop on the lid, reduce the heat to fairly low, and simmer for 10 minutes. Once the wine has reduced almost entirely, and the vegetables are soft, but with a gentle resistance, the dish is ready. Add the remaining butter in cubes and allow it to melt over the vegetables. Serve the asparagus and leeks with pieces of prosciutto draped in and amongst.

Roasted Radicchio and Figs with Stilton and Balsamic Onions

Radicchio, the Italian cousin of Belgian endive, is incredibly bitter. Bitter enough, in fact, to bring a grimace to even the hardest-faced folk. But fear not, for when you roast this ruby-red leaf, the flavor mellows and becomes slightly peppery. Layer that with pungent cheese and sweetly sour vinegar, and you have something very special indeed.

SERVES
4

Preheat the oven to 400°F.

Remove the outer leaves from the radicchio and cut it, through the root, into eight wedges. Arrange these in a medium-sized roasting dish.

Peel the onion and cut it into four wedges, leaving the root intact on each piece. Slice one piece as finely as you can manage—the sharper the knife, the better. Put the slices into a bowl, pour over the balsamic vinegar, and leave to macerate until required.

Slice each of the remaining three quarters of the onion into four slivers and, it bears repeating, leave the root on each sliver, so that the onion layers hold together in each chunk. Put these into the dish with the radicchio. Quarter the figs and add to the dish, then pour over 3 tablespoons oil, and add a generous pinch of salt and pepper. Toss everything together and roast for 15 to 20 minutes, until the onions are fairly soft, the radicchio is wilted, and the figs are mushy.

Crumble over the Stilton, and return to the oven for a few minutes until the cheese melts. To serve, scatter over the macerated onions.

1 radicchio

1 large red onion

2 tablespoons balsamic vinegar

4 figs

3½ ounces Stilton cheese

olive oil
sea salt flakes
coarse black pepper

Variation
If radicchio isn't available, you could use red Belgian endive. In which case, I'd use two endive roots, slicing each into four lengthwise.

Braised Fennel with Halloumi and Grapefruit

SERVES
2

Halloumi is one of those cheeses that satisfies—it is almost meaty. It's great as a lone snack, but here, with the gentle anise tones of fennel, and the sharp tang from the grapefruit, it makes a refreshing plateful of food. What I love the most about this dish, is how summery and fresh it all looks, though it could, of course, be served at any time of the year.

1 large fennel bulb

2 pink grapefruit

12 ounces
halloumi cheese

2 tablespoons
pine nuts

Small handful of
mint leaves

olive oil
sea salt flakes
coarse black pepper
2 tablespoons boiling
water

Preheat the oven to 400°F.

Remove the stalky fingers and leaves from the fennel—though do save the wispy fronds to use as a garnish. Chop the fennel bulb into about 16 wedges, leaving the root of each intact, pop them into a roasting pan, and toss in 2 tablespoons olive oil, and a pinch of salt and pepper. Add the boiling water to the pan, cover with foil, and cook in the oven for 45 to 55 minutes, or until the fennel has really softened—have a nibble on a piece: if it's not quite soft enough to eat, cook it for a little longer. Once it is cooked, drain the fennel, and allow to cool completely.

When the fennel is cool, peel and segment the grapefruit, and toss together with the pieces of fennel.

Slice the halloumi into roughly ¼-inch thick slices. Heat a skillet over high heat. Once the pan is hot, reduce the heat to medium, and fry the halloumi slices for a minute on each side, or until charred and soft. Remove the halloumi from the pan, and use the same pan to quickly toast the pine nuts—just fry them over high heat, tossing them occasionally, until lightly browned.

Lay the warm halloumi slices atop the fennel and grapefruit, scatter over the mint leaves, pine nuts, and reserved fennel fronds, and finish with a good drizzle of olive oil.

Squash, Gorgonzola, and Arugula Spanakopita

Spanakopita, the classic Greek pie made with feta and spinach, is undoubtedly hard to compete with. My version here is totally off-piste in terms of flavor, but it is made, somewhat reassuringly, in the same way. And—dare I say it—I think this updated version gives the original a run for its money.

SERVES
4 to 6

Preheat the oven to 400°F. Lightly grease an 8-inch layer cake pan.

Peel the butternut squash and chop into ¾-inch chunks, discarding the seeds and pulp. Put the chunks into a baking pan, and add 2 tablespoons olive oil, and a generous pinch of salt and pepper. Toss to coat well. Roast for 45 minutes until softened, then transfer to a heatproof mixing bowl to cool.

Meanwhile, heat 1 teaspoon olive oil over high heat in a large saucepan. Add the arugula—you may need to do this in batches—and stir-fry until completely wilted. Allow to cool until cold enough to handle, then put into a clean dishtowel, and squeeze out every last drop of moisture. Add to the roasted squash and mix together. Pull the cheese into small chunks, and add to the bowl along with the eggs and a pinch of salt and pepper. Mix until everything is well incorporated.

In a saucepan, heat the butter over high heat until melted—don't let it brown. Unroll the sheets of phyllo pastry. Paint one sheet with a little melted butter and lay that, buttered-side-up, into the cake pan, allowing the surplus to overlap the sides of the pan. Repeat with the remaining sheets, laying each at a different angle to the next, so that the entire pan is covered. Pile the filling into the pan, squashing it down lightly. Fold the surplus pastry up and over it to conceal it entirely, then paint with the remaining butter. Bake for 30 minutes, until the top is lightly golden and crispy.

This is great served warm or cold, but I would recommend you let it cool for 15 minutes or so. That way, the eggs set, and the flavors mingle. You can cut it into small diamond shapes to serve, but I prefer a hearty triangular wedge.

26 ounces butternut squash (about 1 small squash)

1¼ pounds baby leaf arugula

6 ounces Gorgonzola cheese

2 extra large eggs

3 phyllo pastry sheets

olive oil
sea salt flakes
coarse black pepper
scant ¾ stick unsalted butter

Gochujang Roasted Squash

SERVES
2 to 4

There is a wholesome balance to Asian flavors. Really, it's known as umami—that mouth-filling savoriness. Gochujang, which is a paste made from fermented chiles and soybeans, certainly delivers on the umami front. It's also rather spicy, which, when coupled with the sweet squash, is beautiful.

1 large
butternut squash

3 heaping tablespoons gochujang (hot pepper paste)

2 tablespoons light soy sauce

3 scallions

Small handful of mint

olive oil
coarse black pepper

Preheat the oven to 400°F.

Peel the squash and cut it in half lengthwise. Remove and discard the seeds, then slice the squash along the length into pieces about ½ inch in thickness. Put the squash slices into a mixing bowl and add 1 tablespoon olive oil, a generous pinch of black pepper, the gochujang, and soy sauce, and toss until well coated. Tip out onto a baking pan and bake for 45 to 50 minutes, or until the squash pieces are softened and ever so lightly charred—you can take them even further if you're partial to something a little more crispy.

Finely chop the scallions and mint, scatter over the squash, then serve.

Variation

If you can't get your hands on squash, just use about 3 large sweet potatoes instead, cutting them into long, thin wedges.

Leftover ingredient

The gochujang goes so well in a sweet, store-bought barbecue sauce. Just mix the two together at a ratio of 1:1, and use as a spicy dip for chicken and barbecued meats.

Brazil Nut and Gruyère Pesto with Shattered Lasagne Sheets

SERVES
4

With such reliably fabulous jarred varieties available, so many people rarely make their own pesto, but this version just isn't something you can find in the shops. The Brazil nuts give such a different flavor—obviously more nutty— and seem, in a way, to make the idea of pesto and pasta a much more wholesome affair.

For the pesto, grate the Gruyère and simply blitz it with the nuts, basil, and peeled garlic in a food processor until everything is blended. Then, with the processor still running, slowly pour in the olive oil. You should end up with a fairly smooth pesto.

Bring a large pan of water to a boil and add a large pinch of salt and 3 tablespoons olive oil. Smash the lasagne sheets into uneven shards, and add to the water. Boil for 9 minutes, then drain—but reserve ¼ cup of the starchy pasta water.

Return the cooked pasta to the pan, and add the pesto. Heat over medium heat for just a minute, until everything is warmed through. If at this stage the sauce looks a little scant or too thick, splash in some of the reserved water to loosen— though not too much. Serve the pasta with an extra drizzling of olive oil, and a few chopped Brazil nuts.

1½ ounces
Gruyère cheese

½ cup Brazil nuts,
plus extra to garnish

3 ounces basil leaves

2 garlic cloves

14 ounces
lasagne sheets

⅔ cup olive oil, plus
extra for drizzling
sea salt flakes
coarse black pepper

Crab, Apple, Radish, and Wasabi Pea Salad

White crabmeat just longs to be matched with fresh, slightly sharp ingredients. This salad is so refreshing, but filling, especially if served to fewer people as heartier portions. I adore how the crabmeat flakes into tiny white fronds and floats on top of the perfectly round, razor-thin slices of apple and radish.

This salad might sit ok in the fridge for a few hours, but the apples will inevitably start to oxidize and turn brown, so it's best to make this just before you want to serve it.

2 Royal Gala apples

8 radishes

juice of 2 small limes

14 ounces cooked white crabmeat

¾ cup wasabi peas

sea salt flakes

Using a mandoline—or a sharp knife and a straight eye—cut the apples and radishes into very thin slices. Arrange the slices randomly on a large platter, squeeze over half of the lime juice, and sprinkle with a pinch of salt.

Scatter the crabmeat over the top of the apple and radish slices, then squeeze over the remaining lime juice—if the limes are particularly yielding, perhaps don't use all of the juice; you want this to be balanced, and not too acidic.

Blitz the peas to a rough rubble in a food processor, or put them into a ziplock bag, and bash them with something hard. Sprinkle the peas over the salad and serve.

Miso and Lime Scallops with Soba Noodles

Speed and, of course, flavor, are the main virtues of this dish. It's as wonderful tasting, as it is simple and speedy to make. The miso delivers a certain punchy savoriness that is so well balanced with the sweet and sour honey and lime. Soba noodles are optional—any noodle would do—but I particularly like the nuttiness that the buckwheat flour gives.

SERVES 2

For the soba noodles, it's probably best to follow the package instructions to cook them, which is probably along the lines of: plunge into a pan of boiling water, and cook for 5 minutes. Drain the noodles and set aside until needed.

To make the sauce, simply stir together the miso paste, lime juice, and honey in a bowl. Have this handy at the stove.

Heat 1 tablespoon oil in a skillet over medium heat. Once the oil is hot, add the scallops to the pan. Cook them for a minute on each side, then throw in the sauce and stir to coat. When cooking scallops, don't try to yank them off the bottom of the pan; when they're ready to be flipped, they will allow you to turn them.

Pile the noodles onto a large plate and top with the cooked scallops and sauce, adding a pinch of salt and pepper.

7 ounces soba noodles

6 tablespoons miso paste

4 teaspoons lime juice

1 teaspoon honey

6 sea scallops

olive oil
sea salt flakes
coarse black pepper

Red Curry Sea Bass with Potato Rosti

It's somehow reassuring that the coupling of fish and potato can take many different forms—each totally different—yet remain somehow familiar. This dish, unlike the deep-fried Friday-night version, is incredibly light, and that's thanks to (apart from the lack of batter) those bold spices in the red curry paste, along with the fresh lime and cilantro.

SERVES
4

Preheat the oven to 400°F.

Peel the potatoes before coarsely grating them into a clean dishtowel or cheesecloth. Add a generous pinch of salt and pepper to the potatoes, tossing it through, then squeeze the towel as tightly as possible to remove all of the excess moisture from the spuds. Divide the potatoes into four portions.

Heat 3 tablespoons oil and the butter in a large skillet over high heat. Once the fat is hot, reduce the heat to medium. Form the potatoes into four very tightly compacted patties—pressing the rosti down into a chef's ring with a spoon would make far more sense, but I appreciate that equipment may be limited. Fry each of the rosti for 2 to 3 minutes on each side, then drain on a piece of kitchen towel, and allow to cool for a few minutes.

Score the skin side of the fillets with four or five slashes, and put them into a mixing bowl. Coat the fish fillets in the red curry paste, along with a splash of oil and a pinch of pepper. Once they are well coated, place the fish onto a baking pan, along with the potato rosti, though don't overcrowd the pan; if you have to use 2 baking pans, do so. Roast for 12 to 15 minutes, until the fish is cooked through.

Serve the fish atop the rosti, scattered with some chopped cilantro, and a good squeeze of lime juice.

Leftover ingredient
Use leftover red curry paste for the Sweet Potato and Lentil Red Curry Soup on page 39.

---

2 large baking potatoes

---

4 sea bass fillets

---

3 tablespoons red curry paste

Small handful of fresh cilantro

---

1 lime, cut into wedges, to serve

---

sea salt flakes
coarse black pepper
olive oil
½ stick butter

Cod with Pineapple Salsa

SERVES
4

In Los Angeles, I had the best fish tacos, served with a mango salsa. The combination of meaty white fish, and the spicy, sweet and sour salsa was bizarre, but beautiful. This recipe is inspired entirely by that meal, but I find the pineapple to be an improvement: it isn't as sloppy as the mango, and so delivers that necessary sweetness with a good crunch. I have to follow the dish immediately with a tequila shot—any excuse.

½ medium pineapple

2 fat red chiles

juice of 2 large limes

small handful of
fresh cilantro

4 cod fillets

sea salt flakes
coarse black pepper
olive oil

For the salsa, peel and core the pineapple and chop into small chunks, finely dice the chiles—I don't bother to seed—and add both to a bowl with the lime juice. Finely chop the cilantro, and add to the salsa with a pinch of salt and pepper. Toss together, and leave to macerate while you cook the cod.

Heat a skillet over medium–high heat and add 1 tablespoon oil. Sprinkle a little salt and pepper over the cod fillets, and place them, skin-side-down, into the pan. Fry the fillets for 3 minutes, then flip them over and fry on the other side for an additional 3 minutes. Remove the fish from the pan, and allow to rest for a minute or two, before serving underneath a generous amount of salsa.

Mackerel and Beet Salad

SERVES
4 to 6

This is a salad of opposites. The oily fish is a total contrast to the sweet beets, and the raspberry vinegar is just another disparate element. But put all those elements together, and you have harmony. The sharp vinegar cuts through both the oiliness of the mackerel, and the earthy sweetness of the beets. Dill is the ultimate counterpart to mackerel, and the beets and the hazelnuts offer something crunchy.

**4 medium beets
(a variety of colors
works well)**

**10½ ounces
cooked or smoked
mackerel fillets**

**3 tablespoons
raspberry vinegar**

Small handful of dill

**⅔ cup blanched
hazelnuts**

sea salt flakes
coarse black pepper

Preheat the oven to 400°F.

Wrap the beets individually, skins on, in foil, and roast for 45 minutes. Remove from the oven, and allow to cool completely. Once they have cooled, peel the beets and slice as thinly as possible—using a mandoline would make this much easier.

Arrange the beet slices on a large platter, and sprinkle over a pinch of salt and pepper. Flake the mackerel into mouthful-sized pieces, and arrange over the beets. Drizzle over the vinegar, and roughly chop the dill before sprinkling it on top of the salad.

Heat a dry skillet over high heat, and once it is hot, add the hazelnuts. Fry them, shaking the pan every few seconds, for just a minute or so—when you can smell the aroma of the toasting hazelnuts, they will be ready. Chop them roughly, and scatter them over the salad.

Variations

For an express version of this salad, you could use ready-cooked beets. If you can't get hold of raspberry vinegar, balsamic would be a suitable alternative.

Ginger and Lime Spatchcock Cornish Game Hens

SERVES
2

While a roast chicken is hard to compete with, these miniature versions are strong contenders: each person gets a full bird each, so it feels particularly fulfilling and grand. The trick to getting a lusciously golden, crispy-skinned game hen, is to fry it before smothering it in sauce and roasting it. You could serve this with rice, but for me, one of these on its own is just about enough. I like to tear the flesh from the bones and dunk it into the sauce—using my fingers, of course.

2 Cornish game hens

1 finger-sized piece of fresh root ginger

heaping ½ cup honey

3½ tablespoons light soy sauce

1 lime

coarse black pepper
olive oil

To prepare the game hens, untruss them, and remove the backbones with a sharp pair of kitchen scissors or a knife—cut to one side of the spine, from the parson's nose up to where the head would have been, and then repeat on the other side. Discard the backbone, lay the hens, skin-side up, on a work surface,. and press heavily on the breastbone to flatten out the birds. Set aside until needed.

Preheat the oven to 400°F.

For the sauce, peel and finely grate the ginger, then add it to a saucepan with the honey, soy sauce, zest and juice of the lime, and a pinch of pepper. Bring to a boil, stirring to mix well, then remove from the heat, and set aside until needed.

Place a large, ovenproof skillet or shallow Dutch oven over high heat, and add 1 tablespoon oil. Once the oil is hot, add the game hens, skin-side down, and reduce the heat to medium. Cover with a piece of parchment paper, and weigh down with something heavy—another pan works well; the idea is to keep the birds as flat as possible. Fry for 5 minutes, then flip them over (discard the parchment paper). Pour over the sauce, and roast in the oven, uncovered, for 10 to 15 minutes, or until cooked through, and the top is burnished and bubbling.

Variation
If you can't get hold of Cornish game hens, just use 4 skin-on, bone-in chicken thighs, frying those for only 3 minutes, before smothering in the sauce and roasting.

Duck Breast with Carrots and a Blueberry Hoisin Sauce

One thing that really surprises me is just how very few people have ever fried a duck breast. And when I ask them why, it's not because they don't like duck, but because they don't know how to cook it. The truth is, if you can fry a steak, you can fry a duck breast—it's just as easy. The trick is to just render down the fat first, which will give you a golden, crispy skin, but that takes no effort whatsoever.

SERVES
2

Preheat the oven to 425°F.

Put the carrots, well spaced, onto a baking sheet or pan. Add 1 tablespoon oil, and a pinch of salt and pepper, then toss together with your hands so they are all well coated. Roast for 25 to 30 minutes, until wrinkled, and only very slightly charred.

Score the skin and fat of the duck breasts in a criss-cross pattern, then rub a little salt and pepper into the cuts. Heat a dry skillet over medium–low heat, and once it is hot, add the duck breasts skin-side down. Allow the gentle heat to render the fat down very slowly for 15 to 20 minutes. As the molten fat seeps into the pan, keep pouring it out into a mug or bowl. Once the skin of the duck is deeply golden and crispy, remove it from the pan.

Increase the heat of the pan to high, and as soon as it is hot, add a splash of duck fat and the butter. Place the breasts, skin-side up, into the pan. Cook them quickly, basting the tops with the hot fat and butter—tilt the pan slightly, and scoop up the fat with a spoon, pouring it over the meat. Fry for just 2 minutes, then place the breasts onto a plate, but don't cover them with foil—that will just ruin the crispy skin.

Pour the fat out of the pan, then add half of the blueberries along with the hoisin sauce and half of the lime juice. Cook over medium heat until the blueberries break down to a thick, purple liquid, then add the remaining blueberries and stir to coat them in the juice. Remove from the heat and taste the sauce—if it needs more salt, pepper and/or lime juice, add accordingly.

Lay the duck breasts on top of the roasted carrots, spoon over the sauce, and serve immediately.

9 ounces long baby carrots (I like the ones that still have a little sprig of their tops)

2 duck breasts

¾ cup blueberries

1 tablespoon hoisin sauce

juice of 1 lime

olive oil
sea salt flakes
coarse black pepper
½ stick unsalted butter

Ham and Fennel Pasta

Most would ordinarily assume fennel is best paired with fish, but that's not always the case; it's extremely versatile. Roughly chopped and thrown underneath a chicken before roasting, it softens and gently imparts flavor into the meat. Slowly fried, like onion, it sweetens, and it retains its gentle anise flavor, which is delicious in this creamy pasta sauce with meaty nuggets of ham.

SERVES
2

Slice the fennel as finely as possible—I do this on a mandoline, but it can be done with a sharp knife if you protect your fingers. Save the wispy fronds to garnish. Add the sliced fennel to a large saucepan along with the butter, and set over medium heat. Add a generous pinch of salt and pepper, and stir until everything starts to sizzle. Reduce the heat to low, and cook, stirring occasionally, until the fennel becomes extremely soft—a good 25 minutes.

Tear the ham into bits, add it to the pan, and stir to coat. Pour in the cream, and grate in the Parmesan. Stir until the cheese melts, and you have a smooth sauce, then remove from the heat.

Bring a pan of water with a generous pinch of salt to the boil. Add the pasta, then cook for 9 minutes until tender with just a little bite, then scoop out ⅔ cup of the cooking water before draining the pasta. Return the drained pasta to the pan with the sauce, and heat until warmed through, stirring in the reserved water if it looks a little dry. Serve immediately, and don't forget to scatter over those fennel fronds.

2 medium fennel bulbs

6 ounces cooked ham

scant 1 cup light cream

⅔ cup Parmesan cheese

7 ounces large pasta (I use lumaconi pasta shells)

scant ¾ stick unsalted butter
sea salt flakes
coarse black pepper

Lamb Cutlets with Potatoes, Figs, and Sherry

It's so true that the meat closest to the bone is the most succulent. That's precisely what I adore about lamb cutlets: they are small nuggets of tender meat that just long to be nibbled on. Of course, if you prefer, you could make this with the slightly larger lamb chop, but you'd need to fry it for a minute or so longer on each side.

The fig and sherry combination is inspired by a tapas snack I ate in northern Spain years ago on a college trip. They called it "higos rellenos" (stuffed figs), and although it was a sweet dish, that delicious marriage of figs and sherry is precisely what I loved with the lamb.

20 new potatoes

3 sprigs of rosemary

10 fresh figs

8 lamb cutlets

¼ cup Amontillado sherry

olive oil
sea salt flakes
coarse black pepper

Preheat the oven to 400°F.

Quarter the potatoes, and scatter them over a roasting pan along with a good glug of olive oil, and a teaspoon each of salt and pepper. Add the rosemary sprigs, and toss everything together. Roast for 30 minutes, then halve the figs, add them to the pan, and roast for an additional 15 minutes.

Meanwhile, fry the lamb: rub about 1 tablespoon olive oil and a good pinch of salt and pepper into the cutlets. Heat a skillet over high heat, and once it is hot, add the cutlets, turning the heat down to medium. Fry for 4 to 5 minutes on each side. When the cutlets are cooked, transfer them to a plate, and cover them with foil, then add the sherry to the pan (still on the heat) and stir to deglaze it and get all those meaty bits from the bottom of the pan. Allow the liquid to bubble up and reduce a little, add the juices from the rested meat, then remove the pan from the heat.

Serve two cutlets per person with a hearty portion of the potatoes, five fig halves each, and a good drizzle of the sauce.

Butterflied Lamb Leg with Eggplant, Yogurt, and Golden Raisins

A roasted hunk of lamb is an impressive thing, but it really couldn't be easier to cook—especially when the leg has been butterflied. This is something you can do yourself—just carefully run a sharp boning knife down and around the bone, freeing it from the meat—but, frankly, the butcher will do it in seconds for you.

Naturally the meat will be fairly uneven in width from one end to the other, so do bear that in mind when carving pieces, particularly for the fussy "well-done fiends."

SERVES
6 to 8

Preheat the oven to 425°F.

Make a rub for the meat by mixing 1 tablespoon oil with 2 teaspoons each of salt and pepper, and the hot smoked paprika. Rub this into the lamb leg, then place it, skin-side up, into a large roasting pan, and leave to marinate while you prepare the eggplants.

In another roasting pan, simply rub the whole eggplants all over their skins with 1 tablespoon olive oil, and sprinkle with a little salt and pepper.

Roast the eggplants for 45 minutes and the lamb for 30 minutes. Though if you like your lamb particularly rare, you can pluck it out 5 minutes before that. The eggplants should be blackened somewhat, and looking a little limp. Cover the lamb with foil, and leave to rest until needed.

When the eggplants have cooled enough to handle, peel away the skins, then tear the flesh into long strips. Arrange these in a starburst pattern on a plate. Put the butter into a small saucepan, and place over high heat. Once the butter starts to foam like the head of a cappuccino, and smells nutty, pour it over the eggplants. Drizzle over the yogurt, and scatter over the golden raisins to serve. Slice the lamb thickly, and plate up, drizzling over the meaty juices.

3¼ pounds
butterflied lamb leg

2 tablespoons hot
smoked paprika

4 eggplants

scant ½ cup
plain yogurt

heaping ½ cup
golden raisins

olive oil
sea salt flakes
coarse black pepper
3 tablespoons unsalted
butter

MANY
PLATES

DIPS, SALADS, AND THINGS TO SHARE

One of my worst nightmares is turning up to a party where there isn't a scrap of food in sight—I've ostracised family members for far smaller misdemeanors. I'm not misguided or demanding— I don't expect more than a few dry, gristly canapés at a swanky drinks party; though if that is the case, you can guarantee that I'll be the first to leave in famished pursuit of a burger bar or kebab house. And most likely harboring a swiped bottle of bubbly, stashed in the arm of my overcoat, as compensation!

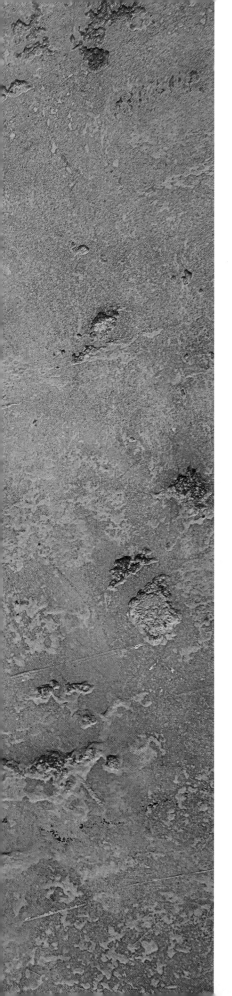

The way I see it is this: if life's major landmarks and milestones can be catered for, so can—and should be— any coming together, no matter how small. If families can provide buffets for a funeral wake when in the midst of mourning, there's no excuse for day-to-day life not to be catered for, too. It's all, in my eyes, part of a lifelong celebration. That may seem a crass argument, but food, ultimately, is life. In the main introduction to this book I noted that "we've long since moved on from the primitive notion of food as fuel," and that's because food is not just for the body, but also for the soul. It's a sickly cliché, but I find it works. Food keeps us living, but good food keeps the party alive.

With that in mind, I wrote this chapter. The purpose here isn't to provide a load of recipes for those larger milestone occasions, but to give you some ideas for food for everyday celebrations. That could simply be a solitary lunchtime at home—though perhaps just one or two of these dishes would suffice in that instance. A night in with friends, and a bottle or two is the perfect excuse to put on a spread, as is an evening with all the family together at home at last.

But it's subjective: whatever your cause to celebrate, these recipes can be easily put together with little fuss. And as you dig into these plates, surrounded by those you love, your cheeks rosy from merriment (and perhaps pilfered booze!), somewhere inside your head a little voice will tell you: it's "bloody good" to be alive.

Cidery BBQ Ribs

A huge plate o'ribs will always signal the start of a feast. That refreshing informality of nibbling, with sauce-sodden fingertips, is what breaks the silence.

Often, ribs take hours of slow cooking, but here they're poached in cider, which speeds up the whole process. The added benefit of the cider is that this imparts a sour, apple-y tang to the meat; and if that's not enough, the acid tenderizes the meat, too.

SERVES
4 to 6

Pour the cider into a fairly capacious saucepan, and add a teaspoon of salt and the ribs. Bring to a boil, reduce to a simmer, and cook the ribs for 25 minutes, skimming off the foam twice during cooking. Drain, reserving ⅔ cup of cider.

4½ cups dry hard cider

For the sauce, put the ketchup, the reserved cider, the Worcestershire sauce, sugar, and 1 teaspoon each of salt and pepper into a medium saucepan, and stir to combine. Bring to a boil, then reduce to a simmer, and cook for 10 minutes, or until thickened—you don't want it be very thick, just thick enough to coat the ribs and stay there.

3¼ pounds pork ribs

heaping 1 cup tomato ketchup

When the sauce is ready, coat the ribs well with it—I use a heatproof pastry brush. Don't throw the leftover sauce away.

¼ cup Worcestershire sauce

Preheat the oven to 475°F.

¼ cup dark brown sugar

Place the ribs on a baking sheet and roast for 15 minutes, basting with sauce halfway through. When the ribs come out of the oven, paint with the remaining sauce and serve.

sea salt flakes
coarse black pepper

Mexican Party Corn

SERVES
8

Mexicans sure know how to party—and I'm not referring to the tequila here (though we all know a party fueled with tequila is sure to get merry and messy!). Mexican food is awesome: the flavors are bold and brash, and everything is prepared with love, but without fuss.

Elotes (corn on the cob) is a particularly popular Mexican street food. The boisterous mixture of cheese, lime, and paprika marries so well with the sweet, toothsome corn. Ordinarily this is prepared on a barbecue, but I prefer the all-season oven method.

4 corn on the cob (buy the ready-peeled variety)

1 large lime

1¼ ounces Parmesan cheese

1 teaspoon smoked paprika

Small handful of fresh cilantro

½ stick unsalted butter
sea salt flakes
coarse black pepper

Preheat the oven to 400°F.

Slice the corn in half lengthwise. This is more difficult than you might expect, because those cobs are tough little buggers; the best way is to stand the corn on its end and place a sharp knife on top. With one hand on the handle of the knife, and the other hand flattened and pressing down on the blunt edge of the blade, slowly seesaw the knife down through the cob. Don't try to rush this, and please be careful; no corn is worth loosing a digit for. Place the corn, cut-side down, into a roasting dish just big enough to accommodate all eight halves snugly.

For the marinade, put the juice of the lime and butter into a small saucepan. Finely grate the cheese, and add it to the pan, then heat everything over high heat until it all melts together. The sauce will definitely look curdled, so please don't think you've done something wrong if it does. Pour this mixture over the top of the corn halves, then sprinkle over the paprika with ½ teaspoon each of salt and pepper.

Roast the corn, uncovered, for 30 to 40 minutes—the corn should be tender, and the cheesy marinade slightly charred. Roughly chop the cilantro, and scatter it over just before serving.

Spinach, Artichoke, and Cheddar Dip

SERVES
8

This has to be my favorite dip. That's a bold statement, I know, and not one that I make without due consideration. There's something about the cheesiness of this, paired with the unique flavor of the artichoke.

To make this even simpler than it already is, you could use frozen spinach (obviously defrost it before use), as that would cut out the entire wilting process—not that that's particularly time-consuming.

If there is any dip left over, it reheats beautifully with a quick blast in the microwave, or in a saucepan over medium heat.

9 ounces spinach

1 large red onion

8½ ounces drained artichoke hearts (from a 14-ounce jar or can)

¾ cup evaporated milk

6 ounces Cheddar cheese

olive oil
sea salt flakes
coarse black pepper

First, wilt the spinach: put it into a medium-sized saucepan with a splash of water and set it over high heat. Stirring, cook the spinach down until it is wilted. Scoop it into a clean dishtowel or cheesecloth, and allow to cool until cold enough to handle. Once it is cool, tightly squeeze the cloth to get rid of the excess water—you want the spinach to be really quite dry. Set aside until needed.

Mince the onion, add to the pan with 1 tablespoon oil, and set over medium heat. Stirring occasionally, cook the onion down for a good 10 minutes, until fairly soft, but not colored.

Put the onion, along with the spinach, drained artichoke hearts, and 1 teaspoon each of salt and pepper, into a food processor, and blitz very finely indeed—scrape down inside the food processor with a spatula if the mixture flies up the sides.

Return the mixture to the pan, and add the evaporated milk. Grate the cheese, and add that to the pan. Set over medium heat, and stirring constantly, allow the cheese to melt. Decant into a serving bowl, and dip to your heart's content. I serve this with tortilla chips, carrot slices, and chunks of bread.

Blushing Hummus

SERVES
8 to 10

Hummus has become a famous staple dip across the world. It's easy to prepare, and this version, made with store-bought cooked beets, is somewhat sweeter than the original, and much more colorful. Serve with tortilla chips or vegetable sticks, and your work is done in a matter of seconds.

This really couldn't be a more simple dip to prepare. Just throw ⅓ cup oil, the beets, drained chickpeas (discard the liquid), the juice of the lime, and Worcestershire sauce into a food processor fitted with a blade. Add a hefty pinch of salt and pepper and blitz to a smooth paste.

Serve in a bowl with a drizzling of olive oil, tear over the cilantro, and scatter with grated lime zest.

18 ounces cooked beets

1 (15-ounce) can chickpeas

1 lime

1 tablespoon Worcestershire sauce

Small handful of fresh cilantro

extra virgin olive oil
sea salt flakes
coarse black pepper

Big Bowl o'Spoon Salad

The thing I love the most about this salad is how bejeweled it looks. Even though it's just a pile of everyday ingredients, there is something spectacularly beautiful about this dish, in both appearance and taste. The trick here is to ensure you dice everything as small, but as neatly, as possible; every spoonful should have a good selection of every ingredient on it.

scant ⅔ cup
dried currants

2 large eggplants

18 ounces mixed-
color tomatoes

1 ounce flat-
leaf parsley

1 tablespoon sumac

olive oil
sea salt flakes

Put the currants into a heatproof bowl and pour over boiling water to cover. Leave to soak for 5 minutes or so.

Chop the eggplants into tiny dice, as small as you can humanly manage without turning them to mush. Heat 3 tablespoons of oil in a skillet over high heat, and once the pan and oil are hot, add the eggplant, and stir-fry for just 1 minute, until the pieces are slightly charred. Remove from the heat, and transfer to a salad or mixing bowl.

Dice the tomatoes as finely as possible—again, you don't want to pulp these; the aim is to achieve tiny little chunks. Add to the bowl with a generous pinch of salt, and toss together. Allow everything to macerate for 30 minutes or so.

Just before serving, roughly chop the parsley, and add it to the bowl, along with the sumac. Drain the currants of excess water, and toss them through the salad. Drizzle over a little olive oil if you think it needs it—though the salt should have drawn plenty of juice from the tomatoes.

Focaccia and Infused Oil

A homemade focaccia will always impress. There's something rewarding about bread that you have made yourself, even though it's really exceedingly simple. It feels as though you've achieved something: a creation to be proud of. And, even better, when people devour the loaf with impressed gratitude it's a win-win situation.

SERVES
10 to 12

To make the focaccia dough, toss together the flour with 2 teaspoons salt and the yeast. Add 1¾ cups water (tap water is fine) with 3½ tablespoons of the olive oil, bring together into a very sticky dough, then knead, until the dough is very elastic and smooth. You can battle with this by hand, slapping the dough down onto and around the worktop, but it's so darn sticky, that using a freestanding mixer fitted with a dough hook, and set on medium speed is far easier.

Once the dough is sufficiently kneaded, coat with a little oil, and leave to rest in a warm place until the dough has ballooned up and tripled in volume—up to 1 hour.

While the dough rises, infuse the oil. Finely chop the tomatoes, and put them into a bowl. Slice the garlic cloves finely, and place them into a pan with the remaining scant ½ cup oil, and set over low heat. Allow to infuse for just a minute, then cool slightly, before pouring the oil over the tomatoes. Roughly chop the parsley leaves (chop the stalks finely) and add to the oil with 1 teaspoon each of salt and pepper.

When the dough has risen, oil a medium, deep-sided roasting pan well, and gently tip the dough out into it, being careful not to deflate it too much. Lightly tug the dough into a very rough rectangle, and allow to rise again until almost doubled in size—up to 1 hour.

Preheat the oven to 475°F. Dip your first and middle fingers into flour, and prod holes all over the surface of the focaccia, ensuring you press your fingers right down to the baking pan below. Bake for 25 to 30 minutes, until golden brown and crispy, then remove and leave to cool.

To serve, slice the focaccia into long, thin chunks, and drizzle the infused oil on top.

3¾ cups bread flour, plus extra for dusting

4 teaspoons (two ¼-ounce envelopes) active dry yeast or instant yeast

12 cherry vine tomatoes

3 garlic cloves

handful of flat-leaf parsley

sea salt flakes
1¾ cups water
⅔ cup olive oil, plus extra for greasing
coarse black pepper

My Favorite
Tomato Salad

SERVES
6 to 8

Call me old-fashioned—which this salad most certainly is—but sometimes it's the classics that are most fulfilling. With strongly aromatic tomatoes, and sweetly pungent shallots, this is easily assembled and completely satisfying.

As a rule of thumb, when shopping for tomatoes, I always give them a good sniff. They should have a strong, sweet scent. If they don't smell of anything, leave them on the shelf. You may look a little odd and receive a few inquiring glances, but when you get them on the table, the result is worth it. Any onlookers will be forever doomed to their insipid tomatoes, while you revel in your flavorsome selection.

2 banana shallots

4 tablespoons
sherry vinegar

1 tablespoon
superfine sugar

18 ounces mixed-color
heritage tomatoes

Small handful of
flat-leaf parsley

Sea salt flakes

Slice the shallots as finely as you can manage into very thin discs, and put them into a bowl with the vinegar and sugar. Leave to macerate for a good 30 minutes.

Slice the tomatoes thinly, and arrange them randomly on a large platter. Sprinkle with a generous pinch of salt, then dress with the soaked shallots. Finely chop the parsley, and scatter over the top.

Watermelon, Cucumber, and Strawberry Salad with a Gin Splash

SERVES
6 to 8

Imagine yourself on a hot, humid day: the ice in your drink clatters, as beads of condensation bejewel the glass, mimicking the pricks of sweat on your brow. Now imagine a salad so refreshing, that it bursts with every bite. So refreshing, that one single mouthful cools you instantly. Well, here it is.

Cut the watermelon into thin triangles—each about ⅛ inch in thickness. Hull the strawberries, and slice them thinly. Slice the cucumber thinly, too. Drizzle the gin over the slices. Finish with a small pinch of salt and pepper and toss together. Arrange the slices randomly on a large platter and serve, scattering over the mint leaves. If you leave this for an hour or so at room temperature, it gets even better.

If you're serving this to children and can't bear the thought of slightly tipsy, unpleasant behavior, substitute the gin for freshly squeezed lime or orange juice.

9 ounces watermelon

6 ounces strawberries

¼ cucumber

2 tablespoons gin

about 10 mint leaves, shredded

sea salt flakes
coarse black pepper

Tempura Cocktail Sausages with Hoisin Dip

SERVES
6 to 8

When I was growing up, my parents ran a fish and chip shop, and I was always intrigued when someone asked for a battered sausage—I never liked sausages or batter. But now my palate has matured, the concept truly is a delicacy for me.

This recipe is Anglo-Asian: the battered sausage is certainly British, while the tempura and hoisin dip remind me of the East.

4½ to 5 ounces
tempura batter mix

30 cocktail sausages
(uncooked)

⅔ cup hoisin sauce

1 tablespoon
fish sauce

juice of 1 lime

¾ cup water
6 cups frying oil

To make the batter, tip the batter mix into a mixing bowl, and make a well in the center. Whisking constantly, slowly pour the water into the flour, to create a smooth batter. Leave it to rest for 5 minutes or so.

Heat your oil in a heavy-bottomed saucepan or wok to 350°F—if you have a deep-fat fryer, just use that. If you've neither fryer nor thermometer, the oil will be ready when a cube of bread dropped into it sizzles and floats—though keep an eye on the heat, so that you don't burn everything.

Have ready a large plate, covered with a few layers of kitchen towels, to drain the sausages after frying. Dredge the sausages through the batter, shaking off the excess, then drop them into the hot oil—you might need to do this in batches to avoid overcrowding. Fry for 5 to 7 minutes, until the batter is golden brown and crispy. Spoon them out—a slotted spoon is the best tool for this—and drain on the paper-lined plate.

For the sauce, simply mix the hoisin, fish sauce, and lime juice together and you're ready to dunk and devour.

Middle Eastern Lamb Nachos

SERVES
6 to 8

Real party food is the sort of stuff you just have to keep going back to, emboldened by the booze, and against the judgement of others. That's true in my case, anyway. But these really are sensationally good, and so different from the boring old chips 'n' dips you'd expect to stumble upon at a disco spread.

The idea is, based on the chapter title, that these are for sharing with a crowd, but this recipe would make a lovely midweek supper too.

---

6 pita breads

---

18 ounces ground
lamb (20% fat)

---

2 tablespoons sumac,
plus extra to finish

---

1 small pomegranate

3½ ounces
feta cheese

---

sea salt flakes
coarse black pepper
olive oil

Preheat the oven to 425°F.

Cut the pita breads into bite-sized triangles—I cut each one into about six—and place them, well-spaced, onto a large baking sheet. Once the oven is hot, bake the pita pieces for 15 minutes, until crisped up, and ever so slightly browned. Remove the sheet from the oven, but leave the pita pieces on it to crisp even more as they cool.

In a mixing bowl, mix together the lamb and sumac with 1 teaspoon each of salt and pepper, and 3 tablespoons olive oil—I use my hands to squelch everything together, so that it's all perfectly mixed.

Heat 1 tablespoon olive oil in a skillet—one you have a lid for—over high heat. Once the oil is hot, add the ground lamb and fry, turning once, until lightly browned. Cover with the lid to trap in the steam. Reduce the heat to low, and cook for 15 minutes—the lamb should be flavorful and tender, and there should be a little bit of juice in the pan.

Scatter the pita pieces around the serving plate and scatter the spiced lamb over the top. Top with the seeds from the pomegranate (I slice the pomegranate in half, hold one half cut-side down over the plate, and bash the top side with the back of a wooden spoon, scattering seeds and juice on top of the lamb). Finish by crumbling over the feta, and adding an extra sprinkling of sumac.

Beet and Anchovy Galette

SERVES
6 to 8

I'm a sucker for ready-prepared beets, the kind that dye your hands bright pink, and taste earthy and sweet. Couple that flavor with the punchy saltiness of anchovies, and that somewhat strange herbal quality of oregano, and you've got an instantly gratifying combination.

12 ounces packaged ready-rolled puff pastry sheets (all-butter is best)

18 ounces cooked beets (the kind in vacuum packs)

3½ ounces anchovies from a jar

2 teaspoons oregano, plus a little extra to garnish

1 ounce Parmesan cheese

sea salt flakes
coarse black pepper

Preheat the oven to 400°F.

Unroll the pastry onto a baking sheet and score a ½-inch margin all around the edge with a knife. Slice the beets as finely as possible, and set the slices onto the pastry in neat lines, overlapping slightly, within the scored margin.

Drain the anchovies, and lay them over the beets in criss-crossing lines, then roughly chop and scatter over the oregano, and a pinch of salt and pepper. Bake the galette for 30 to 40 minutes, or until the pastry has puffed up. Finely grate the Parmesan cheese, and sprinkle it, plus a little extra oregano before serving.

Variation
If you're not keen on anchovies, you could swap them for chopped, pitted black olives.

Pickled Cucumbers with Nigella Seeds and Goat Cheese

SERVES
4

Cheese and pickle is, as most of us know, a match made in heaven. This is just a different way of offering that holy union. Served for lunch, or just as a side salad at a feast, the flavor of the nigella seeds with the sweet-sour pickle is intriguing and delicious.

With a potato peeler or mandoline, slice the cucumbers into thin ribbons and arrange them randomly on a large plate.

In a small saucepan, heat the cider vinegar, sugar, and nigella seeds, bringing it to a boil, then simmering gently for just 2 minutes to let the flavors infuse. Pour the pickling liquid over the cucumber slices, sprinkle with a pinch of salt, and allow to rest at room temperature for a good hour.

Carefully crumble the cheese into small nuggets, and scatter over the plate of pickled cucumbers before serving.

2 cucumbers

⅓ cup cider vinegar

3½ tablespoons superfine sugar

1 tablespoon nigella seeds

4 ounces soft goat cheese

sea salt flakes

Variation
Fennel seeds, in place of the nigella, offer a strong anise flavor; though I'd only use 2 teaspoons of these.

SWEET PLATES

CAKES, PUDDINGS, AND DESSERTS

There's a magic to baking that isn't required in general cookery. While both involve the bringing together of ingredients to produce a final something, the two processes are actually incomparable. In cookery, for the most part, the individual ingredients don't span far from their original form: a carrot becomes a roasted carrot; a duck breast becomes a pan-fried duck breast; a leg of lamb remains a leg of lamb. In that process, you are in complete control of how those ingredients will slightly alter. You can adjust the heat of the pan, and you can quickly whip something out of the oven if it's looking a little overdone. When making a stew or soup, you taste and season as you go, and bland dishes can always be rescued with additional splashes of this and that.

But baking isn't quite so reliant on intuition, or a trust in one's own palate: it is a form of alchemy. It's enchanting how a few ingredients can form a beige batter, which in turn will metamorphose into a golden brown, sugar-dusted masterpiece. As part of that sorcery, there is a great mysterious anticipation as to whether the flour, eggs, butter, and sugar you mix together will come out of the oven resembling anything near to a cake. But that's all part of the excitement, because when you find yourself nibbling on a wedge of jam-filled Victoria sponge, you do so with a sense of smugness and pride—I created this. This mysterious quality isn't intended to evoke deep feelings of fear; the process is an exciting one, involving an element of surprise. I suppose that's why cakes—even lopsided sponges with gaudy sprinkles—will always be met with gasps of surprise and marvel.

But aside from the pride and sorcery, it's impossible to deny that baking is a great bringer of comfort. The entire process, from weighing to devouring, takes me back to childhood and the cozy, warming protection of the kitchen and my family.

Caramelized Bourbon and Peanut Butter Crème Brûlée

MAKES
4

A crème brûlée is a relatively small portion of dessert—the pot confines the serving size, unlike a personally portioned wedge of cake—so it should make a long-lasting impression. My version of this classic dish is decadent and delightful in equal measure, with the gentle warming quality of Bourbon, and a sweet nuttiness from the peanut butter.

¾ cup superfine sugar

2¼ cups whole milk

---

2 tablespoons
Bourbon

---

5 extra large
egg yolks

---

scant ½ cup smooth
peanut butter

Preheat the oven to 325°F. Have four ¾ cup (approx.) ramekins and a deep-sided roasting dish ready, and bring a kettleful of water to a boil.

Heat a medium saucepan over high heat, and once it is hot, reduce the heat to medium. Add ½ cup of the sugar to the pan, and let it slowly melt and caramelize—you want a dark amber color. You can stir the sugar as it starts to melt, but don't overdo it as it could crystallize. An easier, but longer, way to get a caramel is to add ½ cup sugar to a cold saucepan with 4 tablespoons cold water. Dissolve the sugar in the water, then set over high heat, and bring to a boil without stirring at all. Allow the water to boil away until the mixture thickens, and becomes the dark amber required.

Once you have made a caramel, reduce the heat to low, and add the milk a drop at a time, whisking well. The cold milk will cause the hot mixture to bubble and spatter, but stand back a little, ignore this, and carry on carefully. If you add the milk too quickly, the caramel will solidify, and you'll need to stir for a while for it to dissolve. Once the milk is incorporated and fairly smooth, add the Bourbon, and bring to a boil, then remove from the heat.

Whisk the egg yolks in a mixing bowl until smooth and pale, then add the peanut butter a spoonful at a time, beating vigorously after each addition using a wooden spoon, as this will be incredibly thick, until smooth. (If you add the peanut butter all in one go, it will be very difficult to get a smooth mixture.)

Swap back to the whisk and add the hot milk mixture, a drop at a time, to the egg mixture while whisking constantly. This does require elbow grease and patience. Remember: it's easier to get any large lumps out while the mixture is still fairly thick; once you've added all the milk it's far more difficult to get a smooth texture. Once it is all incorporated, pass the custard through a fine strainer into a pitcher, then divide between the four ramekins.

Put the ramekins into the deep roasting dish and pour in boiling water so that the surface of the water is three-quarters of the way up the ramekins. Bake for 40 to 45 minutes, until the crème brûlée just trembles ever so slightly in the center. Allow to cool, then cover and refrigerate for 2 hours; though overnight is best.

Before serving, preheat the broiler and sprinkle the remaining ¼ cup sugar over the top of each crème brûlée. Toast the puddings under the broiler, just until the sugar melts and caramelizes. If you have a chef's blowtorch, use that instead of the broiler.

Variation
If you don't drink Bourbon, but have a stockpile of cheap whiskey, rum, or brandy—gifts from thoughtless family members—just use any of those instead.

Rose Water and Nutmeg Pearl Barley Pudding

SERVES
6 to 8

I first had something along these lines in Stevie Parle's Greenwich, London restaurant, Craft. It's bizarre, weird and totally wonderful. It has the reassuring homeliness of a sweet rice pudding, but that's almost contradicted by the otherworldly scent and spice of rose and nutmeg.

½ cup pearl barley

scant ⅔ cup light brown sugar, plus a little extra for topping

2⅔ cups light cream

2 tablespoons rose water (I use the brand *East End*, and it is just right)

1 teaspoon freshly grated nutmeg

Put the pearl barley in a strainer, and give it a good rinse under cold water until the water runs clear. Transfer the barley to a saucepan, and cover with a couple of inches of water. Bring to a boil, then reduce to a simmer and cook for 35 to 45 minutes, or until the barley is plump, and completely soft. You'll probably need to keep an eye on the water level, and top it up if the pan is threatening to dry out.

Meanwhile, mix the sugar with the cream, rose water, and nutmeg.

Preheat the oven to 400°F.

When the pearl barley is ready, drain off any excess water, and pulse it in a food processor into a finer grain. Add this to the cream mixture, and stir well, so that everything is evenly mixed. Pour into a 9-inch pie plate or cake pan (not a loose-bottomed one, for obvious oozing reasons) and bake for 50 to 55 minutes, until thick and set. Remove from the oven, and sprinkle over a little extra sugar while the pudding is still hot.

Fennel Seed Poached Pear with Chocolate Sauce and Caramelized Oats

MAKES
4

Pears and chocolate are a combination that takes me right back to school dinners. Everything else about those sloppy meals—apart from potato croquettes and ketchup—has slipped from my memory, but pears and chocolate are etched merrily into my mind. This is a slightly more mature version, with the fennel seeds offering a gentle licorice tone to it all.

⅓ cup rolled oats

2¼ cups superfine sugar

3 tablespoons fennel seeds

4 Comice pears

5 ounces dark chocolate (80% cocoa solids)

3 cups water

For the caramelized oats, heat a skillet over high heat. Once the pan is hot, add the oats and toss them to toast for just a minute. Add ¼ cup of the sugar, and allow it to melt slowly and coat the oats. Once the caramel is a gentle golden amber, pour the oats onto a plate, and allow to cool and harden.

Put the water, remaining sugar, and the fennel seeds into a saucepan big enough to comfortably fit the four pears. Stir to almost entirely dissolve the sugar. Peel and core the pears, though leave them whole with their stalks intact. Add them to the pan, and set the heat to high. Once the syrup starts to boil, reduce to a gentle simmer and cover the pears with a disc of parchment paper—I just tear a square off, scrunch it up, unwrap it, then tuck it over the pears. Simmer the pears until a knife easily pierces the flesh, but they remain whole and not mushy—about 20 minutes. Remove the pan from the heat, and allow the pears to cool in the poaching liquid for 5 minutes.

Meanwhile, roughly chop the chocolate and put it into a heatproof mixing bowl. Remove the pears from the pan using a slotted spoon and transfer to a plate. Measure out ½ cup of the pear poaching syrup, and bring that back to a simmer. Pour the simmering syrup over the chocolate, leave it for 10 seconds to melt the chocolate, then whisk to a smooth, glossy ganache.

Place each pear onto a plate, pour over a generous glug of the ganache, and sprinkle with caramelised oats.

Waste not, want not
Don't throw away the leftover syrup; it's so beautiful added in moderation to vinaigrettes for salads, or used as cocktail syrup.

Apple Custard Tarts

The real origin of these flaky little morsels is entirely down to my own flakiness. During an afternoon of Portuguese-custard-tart baking I couldn't be bothered to trundle to the shops for more eggs, so I scoured the cupboards in hope. It was either applesauce or wholegrain mustard as an alternative… Without the courage to be quite so daring, I used the applesauce—and I'm truly glad I did.

MAKES
12

Preheat the oven to 425°F, and grease a deep 12-hole muffin pan well.

Dust the worktop rather liberally with confectioners' sugar, then unroll the pastry onto it and sprinkle it with more confectioners' sugar. Roll the pastry back up tightly—you might need to wet the top edge with just a little water, so it sticks and stays rolled. Slice into twelve even discs—I cut it in half, then cut each half in half, then cut those quarters into three chunky discs.

Stand a disc of pastry up on one of its flat cut sides, then squash it down with the heel of your hand. With a rolling pin, roll it out into a disc big enough to tuck messily into the muffin pan. Press it into the pan, lining the muffin hole, and then repeat with the remaining portions of pastry until each hole of the pan is lined. If you're working in a hot kitchen, it might be a good idea to keep the chunks of pastry in the fridge, then once all cavities in the pan are lined, pop the whole pan into the fridge for 10 minutes or so.

Divide the applesauce between the pastry cases. For the custard filling, whisk together the confectioners' sugar and egg yolks until the sugar dissolves, then whisk in the cream until combined. Pour the custard into the pastry cases—I find it easier to put the custard into a pitcher first, then carefully pour it over the applesauce. Leave a fraction of an inch of pastry clear at the top, as the custard will rise quite dramatically.

Bake for 20 minutes. The custard will darken on top and sprout up over the pastry—and please don't worry if the tarts look cracked, it's all part of their charm. Remove the tarts immediately from the pan, and set on a wire rack to cool. Finish with an extra dusting of confectioners' sugar.

⅔ cup confectioners' sugar, plus extra for dusting

12 ounces packaged ready-rolled all-butter puff pastry sheets

1 cup applesauce

5 extra large egg yolks

⅓ cup light cream

oil, for greasing

Eastern Fruit Salad

SERVES
2 to 4

This is so beautiful—both to behold and to devour—that it seems almost otherworldly. It isn't strictly a fruit salad, as it contains confectionery and nuts, but I couldn't care less what the purists say; I'm emboldened by the beauty of this salad. The flavors, as you can imagine, are both light and complex all at once. The mixture of sharp raspberries and sweet Turkish delight contrasts so well with the mellow figs and salted pistachios.

4 fresh figs

2 tablespoons orange blossom honey

1 cup fresh raspberries

heaping ¾ cup salted roasted pistachio nuts

7 ounces lemon and rose Turkish Delight

Preheat the oven to 425°F.

Cut each fig into eight segments, and arrange them in a small roasting dish. Drizzle the figs with the honey, and roast them for just 10 minutes, until softened, then remove from the oven and allow to cool completely in the roasting dish.

Arrange the figs on a large serving plate. Chop some of the raspberries in half—use a very sharp knife so you don't squish them—and scatter these and the whole raspberries in and among the fig segments. Remove the pistachios from their shells, and chop them roughly, then scatter those on the plate, too. Finally, cut the Turkish delight into small nuggets, and add to the plate. Eat immediately.

Amaretto Apricots with Brown Sugar Meringue

Deep, golden-orange apricots are such a delicious fruit. Although their flavor is primarily of sweet nectar, it comes with a faint tartness which I adore. They are so perfectly paired with the almond tones of amaretto, and the mellow sweetness and yielding crunch of a brown sugar meringue.

Preheat the oven to 425°F.

Halve the apricots, remove their pits, and place them cut-side up in a medium-sized roasting dish. Cut the butter into small dice, and scatter it over the apricots. Sprinkle over the liqueur and 5 teaspoons of the sugar, and bake for 20 to 25 minutes, until the apricots soften, and just start to color very slightly.

While the apricots roast, make the meringue. Whisk the egg whites to stiff peaks, then add the remaining sugar a tablespoon at a time while whisking constantly, until you have a very thick, glossy meringue. I do this on high speed in my freestanding electric mixer, fitted with the whisk attachment, but it can be done just as easily with a handheld electric mixer. Fold the slivered almonds into the meringue, being careful not to deflate the mixture.

Once the apricots have roasted, randomly splodge the meringue over the top of them, and sprinkle over more almonds, then return to the oven for an additional 15 to 20 minutes, until the meringue is colored and slightly crispy on top, and a golden satin matte.

Variation
You could experiment with other pitted fruits, but always try to select the firmer options, as watery fruits could turn into a soggy mess in the heat of the oven.

12 fresh apricots

6 tablespoons amaretto liqueur

1 cup dark brown sugar

3 extra large egg whites

⅔ cup slivered almonds, plus extra for sprinkling

generous ½ stick unsalted butter

Blackberry and Bay
Brown Butter Tart

SERVES
8 to 10

Brown butter tarts are heaven. Imagine the butterscotch sweetness of fudge with the dense, rich texture of a brownie, and you're almost there. Encase all of that—if you haven't already passed out in ecstasy—in a golden sweet pastry, and you have something impossibly indulgent. My version welcomes the sharp blackberries and the haunting, lingering flavors of bay. I use dried bay leaves here, but bear in mind that they do quickly lose their flavor when they sit unused in their jars.

The pastry method here is much more American than continental—French traditionalists, look away now. Not only is it a brown sugar pastry, and so is much darker than usual, it's also just squidged into the tart pan rather than carefully rolled out. It makes life a hell of a lot easier.

heaping 1 cup
light brown sugar,
plus a little extra
for sprinkling

4 extra large eggs

2¼ cups all-
purpose flour

3 dried bay leaves

heaping 1 cup fresh
blackberries

2½ sticks unsalted butter,
plus extra for greasing
sea salt flakes

Very lightly grease a 9-inch fluted tart pan.

I make the pastry in my freestanding electric mixer fitted with the paddle attachment, but you could do it with a handheld electric beater—or even a wooden spoon if you're feeling strong! Beat 1 stick of the butter with ¼ cup of the sugar until very smooth and pale. Beat in one of the eggs, incorporating it well, then toss in a pinch of salt and 1½ cups of the flour. Beat to a smooth dough that's a similar consistency to shortbread. As soon as you have a smooth paste, stop beating, and tip it into the tart pan. With your hands, press the pastry onto the base and up the sides of the pan as evenly as possible. Prick the base repeatedly with a fork, then put in the freezer for 1 hour.

Preheat the oven to 375°F.

Once the pastry has become firm, line it with a layer of parchment paper, and fill with ceramic baking beans or rice, all the way up to the top of the pastry wall. Bake blind for 15 minutes, remove the beans and paper, and then return to the oven for an additional 5 minutes. Once the pastry case is baked, remove it from the oven and allow to cool slightly, but leave the oven switched on.

For the filling, cube the remaining 1½ sticks of butter, and place it into a saucepan with the bay leaves. Heat on low until the butter has entirely melted, then increase the heat to medium–high, and allow the butter to brown. It will bubble and spit as the water evaporates, but when it starts to smell like hazelnuts, and you have a thick, fine-bubbled foam on top, it's ready. Pour it into a cold bowl and allow to infuse for 5 minutes or so.

Whisk together the remaining three eggs and ¾ cup of sugar just until the sugar dissolves. Whisk in the last ¾ cup of flour with a pinch of salt, then slowly incorporate the melted butter as you whisk—the mixture should be velvety and smooth. Remove the bay leaves, and pour the filling into the tart case. Dot the blackberries into the filling randomly, and scatter over a little extra sugar. Bake the tart for 35 to 40 minutes, until golden brown, then allow to cool completely in the pan before serving.

Chocolate–Orange Panna Cotta

MAKES
4

I'm always surprised at how many people are afraid to use gelatin. It's as though it would only take one wrong move for the entire kitchen to implode, but it really is such an easy thing to use—especially leaf gelatin. All it needs is 5 minutes or so soaking in cold water, and then it can be dissolved in a hot liquid.

These creamy little puddings are as easy to make as they are delicious to devour, and I just can't resist how they tremble ever so slightly when nudged.

---

8 ounces dark chocolate (60% cocoa solds)

---

2 gelatin leaves

---

2 cups light cream

---

1 teaspoon orange extract

3½ ounces white chocolate

Have four 6-ounce pudding molds at the ready—or use ramekins or mugs. Roughly chop the dark chocolate, and put it into a heatproof bowl. Submerge the gelatin leaves in a bowl of cold water and leave them to bloom—basically they go from being stiff to soft and floppy.

In a saucepan, bring the cream to a simmer. Once it is simmering, add the orange extract, and remove the pan from the heat. Squeeze the excess moisture out of the gelatin leaves, add them to the cream, and stir until they dissolve. Pour the hot cream over the chocolate, and leave it for 30 seconds to melt, before stirring everything together into a smooth, glossy liquid.

Divide the mixture between the pudding molds, allow to cool to room temperature, then cover with plastic wrap, and refrigerate for at least 4 hours, though overnight is best.

If you want to turn out the panna cotta, dunk each mold into a bowl of boiling water for just a few seconds, to just below the rim, before inverting onto a plate. If the pudding doesn't slip out, give the mold a tap or two on the bottom. If it still won't slip out, run a knife around the edge of the panna cotta and the mold, then try again. And if that fails, don't lose your rag—just eat it out of the mold!

Melt the white chocolate in a heatproof bowl over a pan of barely simmering water—don't let the bottom of the bowl touch the water—and drizzle it over the panna cotta.

Lemon and Rosemary Almond Cake

SERVES
8

Lemon drizzle cake (aka poke cake) is one of those cakes that seems to have always been around. There are countless recipes, each with their own twist, but when baked with rosemary, it is particularly delicious. I first tried this combination at the E5 Bakehouse in London—theirs was made with polenta—and I just had to make a version of my own.

Because this is made with ground almonds, it's gluten-free, too. And in the event that there are leftovers (as if!), it will last a good week or so in an airtight tin.

Preheat the oven to 325°F. Grease and line with parchment paper a 9-inch loose-bottomed cake pan.

Separate 5 of the eggs, placing the whites into one bowl and the yolks into another. Put the remaining whole egg into the bowl with the yolks and add 1½ cups of the sugar, and the zest of all three lemons. Whisk the yolks and sugar until the sugar more or less dissolves into the yolks, then beat in the almonds. This will be an almost impossibly thick batter, but that is normal.

Using a clean whisk, whisk the egg whites to fairly stiff peaks. Scoop one third of the egg white into the yolk mixture and beat vigorously to slacken. Gently fold the remaining egg white into the batter, using a spatula or large metal spoon, being careful not to deflate the whites. Pour the batter into the prepared cake pan, and bake for 45 to 50 minutes, until a skewer inserted into the center comes out fairly clean—there may be the odd moist crumb on there, but that's fine.

While the cake bakes, make the syrup. Put the remaining sugar into a saucepan with the juice of all 3 lemons, the water, and the rosemary sprigs. Bring to a boil, stirring. Boil for 1 minute, then set aside until the cake is baked.

As soon as the baked cake comes out of the oven, stab it repeatedly with a skewer, then pour the syrup over the top and leave it to soak in while the cake cools completely, in the pan.

6 extra large eggs

2 cups superfine sugar

3 large
unwaxed lemons

3 cups ground
almonds

2 sprigs of rosemary

3½ tablespoons water

Secret Ingredient Chocolate Fudge Cake

SERVES
10 to 12

Here is a recipe that I just know some purist folks will scoff at but, believe me, this is not a new way of making the densest, most fudgy chocolate cake imaginable. The secret is condensed tomato soup. In fact, chocolate cake made with this special ingredient was one of Sylvia Plath's favorite bakes, and I can honestly see why. The result is so flavorsome and rich; somehow the tomato soup enhances both flavor and texture. It's my new favorite chocolate cake, and one I think is impossible to compete with.

scant 3¼ cups dark
brown sugar

1 cup canned
condensed cream
of tomato soup

4 extra large eggs

2½ cups self-
rising flour

2¼ heaping cups
cocoa powder

2 sticks unsalted butter,
softened, plus extra
for greasing
1⅔ cups boiled water

Preheat the oven to 350°F. Grease two 8-inch layer cake pans—preferably loose-bottomed—and line the bases with neatly cut circles of parchment paper.

I make the batter in a freestanding electric mixer fitted with the paddle attachment, but you could make it with a handheld electric beater and mixing bowl. Cream 1 stick of the butter with 2 cups of the sugar and half the tomato soup—you want to try to break down the sugar as best you can, and get it pretty much entirely dissolved. Add the remaining soup, and beat that in, along with the eggs. If the batter looks curdled here, that's nothing to worry about, just carry on.

Sift the flour and a heaping ¾ cup of the cocoa powder over the batter and beat in, then add 1 cup of the boiled water in a steady thin stream while beating. As soon as you have a velvety smooth cake batter, divide between the two cake pans and bake for 25 to 35 minutes, or until a skewer inserted into the center of each cake comes out clean. The cakes may crack on top, but don't worry at all. Allow to cool for 5 minutes in the pan, then invert onto a wire rack to finish cooling.

While the cakes are baking, make the frosting. Place the remaining ingredients (⅔ cup water, 1¼ cups sugar, 1½ heaping cups cocoa and 1 stick butter) into a saucepan and heat over medium heat, stirring constantly. As soon as everything melts together and the sugar is dissolved, remove from the heat. Allow to cool in the pan.

Once the cakes are cool and the chocolate icing is a thick, spreadable consistency, it's time to frost. Take one cake, place it onto a cake stand or plate and spread roughly a third of the frosting over the top. Place the other cake on top—I always put it on upside down to get a flat top. Spread the remaining frosting over the top and sides of the cake— a small offset spatula is the best tool for this, but the back of a tablespoon would work in emergency situations.

Variation

A light brown sugar would work if that's all you have, but I'd steer clear of using superfine. The darker, wetter sugars add to the fudgy qualities of the cake. And I probably don't need to warn you against the herby varieties of soup…

Nutella Pudding with Caramelized Pretzels

MAKES
6

The real trickery in this pudding is that you can make it with just two ingredients, Nutella and eggs. This isn't my original idea: social media went mad for Nutella cake back in 2012, but I wondered what would happen if I whisked the egg whites before adding them. The result was an inelegant soufflé, and inelegant—but delicious—it shall stay.

⅔ cup superfine sugar

5½ ounces salted pretzels

---

6 extra large eggs

---

16 ounces Nutella

⅔ cup heavy cream

Preheat the oven to 400°F. Have six 6-ounce (approx.) ramekins or pudding molds at the ready, but don't grease them. Have a sheet of parchment paper ready to tip the caramelized pretzels onto.

First get the caramelized pretzels done. Heat a saucepan over medium-high heat, and once it's hot, add the sugar. Allow the sugar to melt, and turn into a caramel—you can stir it as it melts. If you find there are a few lumps of sugar, remove the pan from the heat as you stir those until dissolved. As soon as you have a golden caramel, add the pretzels and stir to coat, then turn out onto the sheet of parchment paper, and allow to cool completely.

Separate the eggs, putting the whites into one mixing bowl and the yolks into another. Add the Nutella to the bowl with the yolks and beat vigorously until smooth—this is far easier with a handheld electric whisk.

Whisk the egg whites in their bowl until stiff and cloud-like. Add a third of the egg whites to the Nutella mixture, and beat in to slacken, then add the remaining egg whites and fold in gently, until completely incorporated. Divide the mixture between the ramekins, filling them completely, then bake for 20 to 25 minutes. You can take these out when they're still slightly runny in the center, but I prefer them completely baked and brownie-like. And don't worry that these rise and crack on top; it is part of their rustic charm.

Whisk the cream to soft, floppy peaks, and spoon over the puddings—it probably won't all fit on in one go, but I like to add more as I eat. Roughly chop the caramelized pretzels and scatter them over the top of the cream.

Coconut Macaroon and Lime Cheesecake

SERVES
10

On one of my particularly greedy afternoons, I was nibbling on a batch of—admittedly, store-bought—coconut macaroons, and thought they were a little dry. I raided the fridge and found cream cheese and lime curd, so I put them both to good use. The idea for this came instantly, and the next day I had to get down to work. The trick to an utterly toothsome macaroon base is to combine the coconut with melted marshmallows before baking. And since marshmallows are a great setting agent, I used them for the filling, too, so there is no need to bake it.

12½ ounces white mini marshmallows

10½ ounces dried grated coconut

heaping 1 cup good-quality lime curd

16 ounces full-fat cream cheese

zest of 1 lime

2 tablespoons water

Preheat the oven to 350°F. Grease and line the base and sides of a 9-inch springform cake pan.

For the coconut macaroon base, put half of the marshmallows into a heatproof bowl with 1 tablespoon of the water. Set over a pan of barely simmering water, and stir until the marshmallows melt into a thick goo. Add the coconut—still over the heat—and stir until well coated in the melted marshmallow. Transfer to the cake pan, and press it over the base and up the sides. I find it far easier when I grease my hands with a little oil, and I prefer a more rustic, uneven edge (see picture). Bake the base for 15 minutes, until golden brown. This will puff up a little, so as soon as it comes out of the oven, press it down gently to compact it. Allow to cool.

For the filling, repeat the marshmallow melting process with the remaining marshmallows, and the remaining tablespoon of water. Once melted, remove from the heat, and beat in the lime curd, then beat in the cream cheese—it's easier to do this with a whisk, but don't whisk to aerate, just vigorously mix until smooth. Pour the filling into the cooled coconut base, and refrigerate overnight. Don't be impatiently prodding this, or prematurely slicing it; just forget about it until it sets completely. Sprinkle over the lime zest before serving.

Mont Blanc Triangle Torte

This is my abstract version of Mont Blanc—both mountain and dessert. The flavor combination makes up the classic French dish, while the form of this triangular, meringue-covered torte represents a snow-topped mountain range. You may think I've made a mistake in using plain flour instead of self-rising, but that is a purposeful selection; if this were an aerated cake mixture, it would be far more difficult to cut and shape.

scant 1 cup
superfine sugar

3 extra large eggs

heaping ¾ cup
all-purpose flour

2 heaping tablespoons
cocoa powder, plus
extra for dusting

9 ounces canned
sweetened chestnut
spread (I use the
Clément Faugier
vanilla variety)

1⅛ sticks unsalted butter,
at room temperature,
plus extra for greasing

Preheat the oven to 400°F. Grease a 10 × 15-inch jelly roll pan and line the base with parchment paper.

Beat the butter until pale and fluffy, either with a handheld electric whisk, or using a freestanding electric mixer fitted with the paddle attachment. Add a scant ⅔ cup of the sugar and stir through to avoid causing a giant cloud of sweet sugar smoke, then beat until well incorporated. Beat in 2 of the eggs until well blended, then beat in the flour and cocoa powder until you have a smooth batter.

Scoop the batter into the jelly roll pan, level off, and bake for 12 to 15 minutes, or until a skewer comes out clean. Remove from the oven, and allow to cool completely in the pan.

Take the torte from the pan and place it horizontally on the worktop before you, then slice it into four equal rectangles— I cut it in half, then cut each half in half.

Spread a quarter of the chestnut spread over one of the torte rectangles. Place another rectangle evenly on top, then repeat until you have four layers of torte, sandwiched together with three layers of filling. Don't worry if the edges don't line up perfectly at this stage. Place into the freezer for 20 minutes to firm up.

When the torte is chilled and firm, take it out of the freezer and carefully trim all four edges to neaten. Place the torte on the worktop, with the layers lying horizontally. With great care and a sharp serrated bread knife, slice the torte in half on a diagonal into two long triangular pieces. I place one of the longer edges of the torte at the edge of the worktop, then I position the blade of my knife on the right hand side of the torte, from the bottom corner (the one nearest to me) to the top corner (the one furthest away from me). Using the edge of the worktop to guide the knife, I gently saw the torte in half. If you're left-handed, start at the left-hand side and saw the knife towards the right.

Align the pieces so that the backs are touching and the stripes of torte are vertical. Spread the remaining chestnut spread on the back of one of the triangles and then stick them together. Chill again for another 20 minutes.

Separate the remaining egg—you can freeze the yolk to use at a later date—and place the white with the remaining 5 tablespoons of sugar into a heatproof mixing bowl. Set the bowl over a pan of barely simmering water, and using a handheld electric beater, whisk until the mixture feels slightly hot and the sugar has dissolved into the egg white. Remove from the heat, but keep whisking until you have a very thick, smooth, and glossy meringue.

Spread the meringue over the sloping sides of the torte, and sprinkle over a light dusting of cocoa powder.

Autumnal Apple Crisp Cake

SERVES
10 to 12

This cake makes an impression, but rest assured that because precision isn't required when it comes to decorating it, the more rustic the Swiss meringue is, the better the cake will look. It does take a little time to get all of the different elements ready, but an afternoon off, dedicated to baking, is never a wasteful occupation.

3¾ cups superfine sugar

---

4 Braeburn apples

---

11 extra large eggs

2½ cups self-rising flour

---

3 tablespoons pumpkin pie spice, plus extra for dusting

---

scant ½ cup water
3 sticks unsalted butter, at room temperature

Preheat the oven to 250°F.

Combine a scant ½ cup of water with ½ cup of the sugar in a saucepan, and bring to a boil. Boil for 1 minute, then turn off the heat. Slice two of the apples finely, using a mandoline—there's no need to peel or core them. Dip the slices into the hot syrup, and leave to soak for 1 minute, then remove, and allow the syrup to drip off them—I lay them on a cooling rack set over a couple of sheets of paper towels to drip dry, just for a minute or two.

Arrange the apple slices, well spaced, on two baking sheets lined with parchment paper. Put into the oven and leave to dry out for 2 hours, flipping the apple slices over after 1 hour. Remove the slices from the oven, arrange them on a dry cooling rack, and leave them to cool and crisp completely.

Increase the oven temperature to 350°F. Grease three 8-inch layer cake pans, preferably loose-bottomed, and line the bases with neatly cut circles of parchment paper.

Beat the butter with 1¾ cups of the sugar until well creamed and fluffy. Add six of the eggs, one at a time, beating well after each addition, then add the flour and mixed spice, and beat until smooth. Peel and core the remaining two apples, chop them into small dice, and fold them through the batter.

Divide the batter between the cake pans as evenly as possible, smooth out the tops with the back of a spoon, and bake for 30 to 35 minutes, or until a skewer inserted into the center comes out clean. Remove from the oven, and allow to cool in the pans for 5 minutes, then invert onto wire racks to cool completely.

For the meringue, separate the remaining 5 eggs, and place the whites into a heatproof bowl along with the remaining 1½ cups sugar—freeze the yolks for another time. Set the bowl over a pan of barely simmering water, and whisk with a handheld electric mixer until the mixture feels slightly warm on the finger. Remove the bowl from the pan, and continue whisking until you have a very thick, smooth meringue.

To assemble, simply place one cake onto a cake stand and spread over some of the meringue. Repeat until you have three layers of cake sandwiched together with two layers of meringue. Spread the remaining meringue over the top and sides of the cake, scraping the meringue away to reveal the sponge layers. Finish the cake by placing the apple slices around the base, then sprinkle over a little mixed spice. If you have a chef's blowtorch you can char the meringue slightly, but it's just as beautiful without.

Self-Saucing Orange Curd Pudding

There's something almost miraculous about a self-saucing pudding: you just throw all of the ingredients together, and it comes out cozily warm, and soaked in a thick, sweet sauce. If you wanted to prepare this in advance, you could. Just make the batter and pour it into the dish, then refrigerate until required—for no more than 2 days, though. Make the sauce fresh, and pour that over the pudding just before baking.

Preheat the oven to 350°F. Grease an 8 × 12-inch baking dish.

For the batter, beat the butter, ⅔ cup water, ½ cup of the orange curd, 1¼ cups of the sugar, the flour, eggs, and grated zest of the oranges until smooth—I do this in a food processor, but a freestanding mixer works fine, as would a wooden spoon and elbow grease. Pour the batter into the prepared dish and refrigerate for 1 hour.

For the sauce, whisk together the remaining orange curd with ¾ cup boiling water, and the remaining ¼ cup of sugar with the juice of one of the oranges. Pour the sauce over the pudding, then bake for 50 to 60 minutes, or until a skewer inserted into the center comes out clean. Do bear in mind there is sauce in this pudding, which will stick to the skewer. Leave to stand for 10 minutes before you dig in.

SERVES
8

1⅔ cups orange curd

1½ cups light brown sugar

2¼ cups self-rising flour

2 extra large eggs

2 oranges

1½ sticks unsalted butter, softened, plus extra for greasing
scant 1½ cups water; ⅔ cup at room temperature, and ¾ cup boiling

Brown Sugar Meringues with Hazelnut-Butterscotch Sauce

MAKES
4

Meringues have been done time and time again, and with very good reason: they're delicious. Nothing quite compares to that crispy outer shell, beneath which lies a pillowy marshmallow center. I remember my mom experimenting with brown sugar in a meringue once, and the result was so chewy and beautifully flavored. Dark brown sugar is somewhat damper than regular superfine, so this recipe uses a Swiss meringue method, the result of which is a little more stable than the usual French meringue.

4 extra large
egg whites

1³⁄₈ cups dark
brown sugar

1½ tablespoons
cocoa powder

⅓ cup hazelnuts

1⅛ cups heavy cream

scant ½ stick unsalted
butter

Preheat the oven to 325°F. Line two baking sheets with parchment paper.

Put the egg whites into a heatproof mixing bowl and add 1⅛ cups of the sugar. Set the bowl over a pan of barely simmering water, and whisk—this is more easily done using a handheld electric mixer. Whisking constantly, allow the sugar to dissolve, and as soon as the mixture feels slightly hot on the finger, remove from the heat, and whisk vigorously until you have a very smooth, stiff meringue—a good 5 minutes or so. Blob 4 large piles of meringue, well spaced, onto the baking sheets and with the back of a spoon morph them into little indented nests. Sprinkle over the cocoa powder, and put the meringues into the oven, reducing the heat to 275°F. Bake for 2 hours, then turn off the oven, and open the door slightly, to allow the meringues to cool and crisp inside.

Heat a dry skillet over high heat, then toss the hazelnuts in the pan for a minute or so, just until gently toasted; they should smell of hazelnuts, but not bitterly so. Chop the toasted nuts roughly, and put them into a bowl.

For the sauce, put the remaining ¼ cup of sugar into a saucepan with the butter and 3½ tablespoons of the heavy cream. Bring to a boil, stirring, and as soon as it's velvety smooth and well mixed, remove from the heat.

To serve, whisk the remaining scant 1 cup of heavy cream until soft and floppy. Spoon the cream over the meringues, then drizzle over the sauce and scatter over the toasted hazelnuts.